The
Connell Guide
to
Jane Austen's

Mansfield Park

by
John Sutherland
and
Jolyon Connell

Contents

How believable is the ending of *Mansfield Park?*   94

What view of the world does *Mansfield Park* leave us with?   99

NOTES

What is *Mansfield Park* about?

Few novels have divided critics more than *Mansfield Park*. It has been fiercely argued over for more than 200 years, and with good reason: it is open to radically different interpretations.

At its broadest, it is a novel about the condition of England, setting up an opposition, as the critic and biographer Claire Tomalin puts it, between someone with strongly held religious and moral principles who will not consider a marriage that is not based on true feeling, and is revolted by sexual immorality, and "a group of worldly, highly cultivated, entertaining and well-to-do young people who pursue pleasure without regard for religious or moral principles".

On the worldly side are Henry and Mary Crawford, tainted by their uncle, the Admiral, who keeps a mistress openly and passes on a light-hearted attitude to vice to his niece, while Maria and Julia Bertram are led astray by vanity and greed, with their corruption completed by a move from the country, where "outwardly correct standards are maintained", to London, where anything goes.

That is certainly one way of looking at *Mansfield Park*: the "parallels with the highest Regency society are all there", as Tomalin says. But while some early readers were pleased by what they saw as the novel's championing of morality, others reacted less warmly, including Jane Austen's highly intelligent mother, who found the virtuous Fanny Price "insipid", and Austen's sister, Cassandra, who wanted Jane to let Fanny marry Henry Crawford.

Many critics have felt the same. In 1917, Reginald Farrer, writing in the Quarterly Review, thought *Mansfield Park* "vitiated throughout by a radical dishonesty". The author, he said, is oppressed by "a purpose of edification" at cross purposes with her natural gift. The Crawfords "obviously have her artist's affection as well as her moralist's disapproval... Fiction holds no heroine more repulsive in her cast-iron self-righteousness and steely rigidity of prejudice" than Fanny. Mary, on the other hand, "would be... most delightful as a wife". Twenty years after Farrer's attack, Q.D. Leavis weighed in with similar misgivings: for all its brilliance, she found *Mansfield Park* "contradictory and confusing" and spoilt by Austen's "determination to sponsor the conventional moral outlook".

This critical attitude found its most vigorous expression in a famous essay by the novelist Kingsley Amis, which appeared in *The Spectator* in 1957. No other of her novels, he argued, embodies to a comparable degree Austen's

> habit of censoriousness where there ought to be indulgence and indulgence where there ought to be censure. These are patently moral 'oughts', and it is by moral rather than aesthetic standards

that *Mansfield Park,* especially, is defective. Although it never holds up the admirable as vicious, it continually and essentially holds up the vicious as admirable...

As social beings, says Amis, Edmund and Fanny are "inferior" to the Crawfords. Henry and Mary are "good fun"; the other two simply aren't. "To invite Mr and Mrs Edmund Bertram round for the evening would not be lightly undertaken." More basically than this, Edmund and Fanny are "morally detestable". He is narrow-minded and pompous, while Fanny's notions and feelings "are made odious by a self-regard utterly unredeemed by any humour". She is, concludes Amis damningly,

> a monster of complacency and pride who, under a cloak of cringing self-abasement, dominates and gives meaning to the novel. What became of that Jane Austen (if she ever existed) who set out bravely to correct conventional notions of the desirable and virtuous? From being their critic (if she ever was) she became their slave. That is another way of saying that her judgement and her moral sense were corrupted. *Mansfield Park* is the witness of that corruption.

In another, highly influential essay, written three years earlier, the American critic Lionel Trilling sought to rehabilitate *Mansfield Park.* Jane Austen herself, when embarking on it, wrote to her sister

Cassandra: "Now I will try to write of something else; – it shall be a complete change of subject – Ordination." Trilling takes her at her word: the idea of ordination runs strongly through his interpretation of the novel, he says. He accepts Fanny's shortcomings – "Nobody, I believe, has found it possible to like the heroine of *Mansfield Park*" – but sees her as a Christian heroine whose "debility" is a sign of her saintliness. The question of ordination is important as it involves a conception of professionalism and duty which looks forward to the Victorians; the episode of the play may seem absurd, but it illustrates the dangers of impersonating others and of not being true to ourselves. The Crawfords are superficially attractive, but they are insincere; Fanny has integrity.

This view is echoed by the leading late 20th century English critic, Tony Tanner. Like Trilling, Tanner sees the novel as without irony; it celebrates stillness, he says; it seems "to speak for repression and negation, fixity and enclosure... in the debilitated but undeviating figure of Fanny Price we should perceive the pain and labour involved in maintaining true values in a corrosive world of dangerous energies and selfish power-play". Fanny "suffers in her stillness. For Righteousness's sake."

Marilyn Butler's important book, *Jane Austen and the War of Ideas* (1975) extends this line of argument, believing Austen, in all her novels, to be making a conservative philosophical case against the dangerous ideology of the French revolution. In Butler's reading, the novel is deeply imbued with the values of Edmund Burke, whose *Reflections on the Revolution in France* (1790) portrayed British society as held together not by reason but by love and loyalty, with the castle or country house a symbol of its strength. Fanny, thinks Butler, is a Christian heroine faced by a series of trials. "Portsmouth is Fanny's exile in the wilderness, her grand temptation by the devil Mammon" in the shape of the rich, estate-owning Henry Crawford. Portsmouth and London must be rejected; peace can only be found at rural Mansfield, which promises a life "of affectionate service, together with an inner life of meditation".

Yet Butler's interpretation, like many in the 1970s and earlier, seems a curiously restricting one. Butler pronounces Fanny a "failure" in a novel which is in essence "a skilful dramatisation of the conservative cause" and makes this bracing claim:

> The theme of *Mansfield Park* is the contrast of man-centred or selfish habits of mind, with a temper that is sceptical of self and that refers beyond self to objective values. Since Fanny is the representative of this orthodoxy, the individuality of her consciousness must to a large extent be denied.

But is this really true? Is Fanny's individual consciousness denied? Modern critics of *Mansfield*

Park see Jane Austen as engaged in an altogether more subtle and subversive task than Butler, Tanner or Trilling allow. The feminist critic Claudia Johnson, for example, argues that the novel "erodes rather than upholds" conservative values and that Fanny Price, for all her happiness at the end, is the unconscious victim – as well as saviour – of the social world into which she is drawn. *Mansfield Park* may seem to endorse Fanny's severity with Mary Crawford, but "it also explodes her confidence in the dispositions of patriarchal figures". The ending of the novel Johnson sees as ironic, with Austen hurrying her characters into tidy destinies which are hard to credit.

Johnson also contends, more controversially, that "the family fortunes [Sir Thomas] rescues depend on slave labor in the West Indies". It's a claim frequently made by modern critics, most influentially by the Palestinian-American Edward Said, in *Culture and Imperialism* (1973). "Follow the money," Said instructed. Where does the wealth which keeps up the magnificence of Mansfield Park come from? Most of it, he asserts, from black slaves, working 3,000 miles away, in the sugar plantations of the Caribbean, in conditions of inhuman exploitation.

According to Said, the Bertrams "could not have been possible without the slave trade, sugar, and the colonial planter class". Their revenues "could only" have been drawn from sugar plantations. Moreover, he asserts, this imperialistic inward flow

9

of capital applies not merely to one family of landed gentry, but to the enrichment of all Britain's genteel classes – even a clergyman's family, resident in rural Hampshire. "Yes," Said concludes, "Jane Austen belonged to a slave-owning society." Just as Georg Lukács instructed that we should insert the "invisible serf" into every scene in Tolstoy, so should the reader sketch in a shackled slave, groaning under the overseer's whip, behind Emma's father, Mr Woodhouse, at Hatfield, as he sups his evening gruel. As for Fanny: she, in effect, is "a transported commodity" who replicates the slave, while Sir Thomas's efficient management of his

FREE INDIRECT SPEECH

Austen is rightly famous for her use of free indirect speech (FIS), the presentation of her characters' thoughts, feelings and unquoted speech in a way which reflects the way they think, feel and speak. For much of *Mansfield Park* the narrative viewpoint, though mostly Fanny's, is promiscuous (though it becomes more narrowly focused on Fanny in Part Three). We are shown the thoughts, feelings, self-deceptions and evasions of Edmund, Mary and other major characters.

In the last chapter, the narrator's mask appears to drop completely: "Let other pens dwell on guilt and misery. I quit such odious subjects as soon as I can..." Before this, the narrator sometimes intervenes, as when describing Mrs Price's loss of Fanny. "Poor woman!

estate on returning from Antigua echoes the authoritarian behaviour of the slave-master.

Said's claims need to be treated with caution. Brian Southam, while accepting the presence of a colonial subplot in *Mansfield Park,* says this aspect of the novel needs very careful analysis. Indicting a whole society as "slave-owning" does not make for a sensible reading of *Mansfield Park.* Mrs Norris blurts out that the family's "means will be rather straitened if the Antigua estate is to make such poor returns" – and Sir Thomas says it would "not be undesirable to [Sir Thomas] to be relieved from the expense of [Fanny's] support". But we have no

---

She probably thought a change of air might agree with many of her children." With this exclamation of sympathy, notes Roy Pascal in his justly praised analysis of free indirect speech, *The Dual Voice,* the narrator acquires something of a personality and at the same time, by using the qualifying "probably", renounces the narratorial right of omniscience.

But frequently our judgements are guided by Austen's brilliant use of FIS. In the first chapter, for example, the narrator makes clear how selfish and hypocritical Mrs Norris is, and how indolent and hesitant Sir Thomas. As they discuss adopting Fanny, free indirect speech (FIS) is used to show how they take refuge in evasions:

> *Sir Thomas could not give so instantaneous and unqualified a consent. He debated and hesitated; – it was a serious charge; – a girl so brought up must be adequately provided for, otherwise there would be cruelty instead of kindness in taking her from her family.*
> *(1)*

The evasions are given in FIS, though when Mrs Norris makes

idea of the extent of his, or Mansfield Park's, dependence on his Antiguan investments, just as we have no idea of the precise reasons for his Antiguan visit. He could be going to quash a slave rebellion, or on a humanitarian mission to improve the lot of a depleted workforce after the abolition of slavery in 1807. We don't know. And we should be careful, says Brian Southam, about filling in the "silences" in Austen's narrative.

But Said's highly politicised reading of *Mansfield Park* was part of a trend. In the last years of the 20th century some form or other of political radicalism was more or less *de rigueur* in academic

---

the case for inviting Fanny her arguments come in direct speech. A little further on, however, when she informs the Bertrams that she can't possibly house Fanny, it is her words, and evasions, that are given in free indirect speech.

> *Sir Thomas heard, with some surprise, that it would be totally out of Mrs Norris's power to take any share in the personal charge of her [Fanny]... Mrs Norris was sorry to say, that the little girl's staying with them, at least as things then were, was quite out of the question. Poor Mr Norris's*

indifferent state of health made it an impossibility: he could no more bear the noise of a child than he could fly; if indeed he should ever get well of his gouty complaints, it would be a different matter. (1)

In the first sentence, the narrator moves towards free indirect speech: the words "it would be totally out of Mrs Norris's power" seem to be hers. After that, with "Mrs Norris was sorry to say" we are in full FIS: we feel the presence of the speaker, though, as with the passage above, the narrator has modified what is said in criticism. This was a time in which post-structuralists sought for the truth of a work of fiction in the "fissures", or "silences", in the text – read between the lines of *Mansfield Park* and you'll find plenty about the slave trade, no matter that generations of previous critics had barely noticed it. Said was far from alone in his interpretation – and up to a point anti-imperialist, anti-slavery readings of *Mansfield Park* went hand in hand with feminist ones; British imperialism, after all, could as readily be blamed on patriarchal values as the subjugation of women.

Yet while we must be wary of imposing our own

what Pascal calls "a subtle, ironical way" by turning the various excuses into a list. "As a result, the reader is made keenly aware of the morally indifferent quality, the evasiveness, the selfishness, of what is said, its lack of authenticity."

An even more complex example of the use of FIS comes when the theatricals are being discussed. Edmund, having failed to persuade his brother to give them up, tries his sisters, Maria and Julia.

His sisters, to whom he had an opportunity of speaking the next morning, were quite as impatient of his advice... as Tom. – Their mother had no objection to the plan, and they were not in the least afraid of their father's disapprobation. There could be no harm in what had been done in so many respectable families, and by so many women of the first consideration; and it must be scrupulousness run mad, that could see anything to censure in a plan like their's, comprehending only brothers and sisters, and intimate friends, and which would never be heard of beyond themselves. Julia did seem inclined to admit contemporary values on Austen's text, clever feminists like Claudia Johnson have been important in redressing the balance. Critics these days are less inclined to view Fanny Price as a mere picture of goodness. "The still, principled fulcrum of moral right, celebrated and excoriated by earlier critics," says John Wiltshire, is now "understood to be a trembling, unstable entity", an "erotically driven and conflicted figure both victim and apostle of values inscribed within her by her history of adoption".

Austen's interest in the psychology and motives of her heroine in *Mansfield Park* is subtle and

---

Maria's situation might require particular caution and delicacy – but that could not extend to her *– she was at liberty; and Maria evidently considered her engagement as only raising her so much above restraint, and leaving her less occasion than Julia, to consult either father or mother. Edmund had little to hope, but he was still urging the subject, when Henry Crawford entered the room, fresh from the Parsonage, calling out, "No want of hands in our Theatre, Miss Bertram".*

(13)

The arguments of Edmund's sisters are given in free indirect speech, to which an abrupt end is put by Henry's intervention, which is in direct speech. What is especially interesting, says Pascal, "is not only the brilliant evocation of the manner in which the girls argue and speak, but the suggestions that what we are reading is Edmund's registration of what they say".

The italicised "*did*" and "*she*" in Julia's argument, and the "evidently" of Maria's, evoke not just the egoistic girls themselves but also the listener, Edmund, as he draws his cautious conclusions. In this penetrating. In part at least, this is a novel about female desire – the plot revolves around the passionate feelings of two young women, Fanny and Maria. The argument that it is a straightforward defence of the conservative way of life is hard to sustain, and few critics nowadays consider it as such; it is equally, perhaps more plausibly, seen as questioning the whole patriarchal basis of society, and in particular the way and the extent to which women were trapped by a system over which they had no control. Far from being devoid of irony, it is now frequently, and perhaps rightly, thought of as the most ironic of all Austen's novels.

---

passage it is as if it is Edmund himself reporting the sisters' arguments and "sifting and arranging them, in order to be able to cope with them". The words in italics may bear Julia's emphases in the first place, but they also bear Edmund's – the word "evidently" makes this clear.

With its clever use of FIS, this passage is full of irony. We see, says Pascal, how Edmund understands the "frivolous and selfish characters" of his sisters, "and we can infer throughout the novel that he knows much more than his words, his explicit thoughts, or his behaviour inform us of".

"*Mansfield Park* departs from the mode of all preceding novels in its deliberately shifting, serial, roving representation of consciousness," says John Wiltshire. The "anchoring focus" is Fanny Price, but we are also made aware of the inner purposes and reflections of Sir Thomas, Maria, Mary, and Tom as well as Edmund. "Through the adoption of distinct perspectives the novel generates a kind of structural or endemic irony: one person's project or desire immolates them, and puts them, unknowlingly, at cross purposes with another's." ▪

Why does Fanny behave as she does?

The critic David Lodge maintains that for *Mansfield Park* to work as a novel we have to identify with the heroine. This is debatable, but if true then Fanny's physical weakness and her passivity have always posed a problem. She is not the kind of girl male readers fall for. The emphasis on her physical frailty – on how "debilitated" and "enfeebled" she is – sets her apart from Austen's other heroines and especially from her immediate predecessor, Elizabeth Bennet, whose boundless energy and love of muddy walks bewitches Darcy as it has bewitched generation of readers.

Fanny is also the only Austen heroine whose childhood is described in detail. Neglected by her parents, she arrives, aged 10, at Mansfield, where her small size and lack of vigour are thrown into relief by her cousins – "a remarkably fine family, the sons very well looking, the daughters decidedly handsome, and all of them well-grown and forward for their age".

Miserable at first, it is hardly surprising she clings to Edmund, the only cousin who treats her kindly and who fills the gap left by William, the brother she loves and has had to leave behind (William himself being a substitute for the neglectful mother). With Edmund, Fanny forms what has been aptly called an "anxious attachment".

Fanny's love for Edmund, says John Wiltshire, "shapes the novel". It is a love "that is tenacious, possessive and funded by primary psychological urgencies" but it is also a love that has rarely been given the critical attention it deserves.

An exception to this came early, in an essay written in January 1821 by the clergyman Richard Whately. Whately was interested in what he called the "inward" quality of Austen's depiction of Fanny Price's "heart":

> Fanny is... armed against Mr Crawford by a stronger feeling than even by her disapprobation; by a vehement attachment to Edmund. The silence in which this passion is cherished – the slender hopes and enjoyments by which it is fed – the restlessness and jealousy with which it fills a mind naturally active, contented and unsuspicious – the manner in which it tinges every event and every reflection, are painted with a vividness of which we can scarcely conceive any one but a female, and we should add, a female writing from recollection, capable.

Fanny, says Whately, is portrayed as a sexual being; in an extraordinary breach with the conventions of the day, the novel shows a heroine feeling and even exhibiting uninvited passion. Women in the novel are presented as "liable 'to fall in love first', as anxious to attract the attention of agreeable men..." No authoress but Jane Austen would have dared do anything so bold. It would be a long time, says John Wiltshire, "before the intelligence that is now partly obscured by this young churchman's overtly masculine bias was matched in the criticism of this novel".

In the first part of *Mansfield Park,* Fanny's tender feelings for Edmund gradually turn into adult and sexual passion, but it is necessarily a silent passion. Her status in the household as inferior, as an outsider, rule out its expression, or even Fanny's own consciousness of what is going on. She can never be the equal of Sir Thomas's children, as he makes clear even before she arrives at Mansfield. "Their rank, fortune, rights, and expectations will always be different."

It is Edmund who consoles her in her wretchedness and the way he wins her trust is shown with great subtlety by Jane Austen. As Roy Pascal notes in *The Dual Voice,* when Edmund talks to her about her mother and brothers, her answers are given first in simple indirect speech, then in free indirect speech (imitating her use of language), then finally in direct speech.

On pursuing the subject, he found that dear as all these brothers and sisters generally were, there was one among them who ran more in her thoughts than the rest. It was William whom she talked of most and wanted most to see. William, the eldest, a year older than herself, her constant companion and friend; her advocate with her mother (of whom he was the

darling) in every distress. "William did not like she
should come away – he had told her he should miss
her very much indeed." "But William will write to
you, I dare say." "Yes, he had promised he would, but
he had told her to write first." "And when shall you do
it?" She hung her head and answered, hesitatingly,
"she did not know; she had not any paper." (2) *

Edmund's remarks here are all in direct speech,
hers are first explained by the narrator, then
presented in free indirect speech (though placed in
inverted commas). After this, the pair begin talking
in direct speech. "The psychological effect is
marked," says Pascal.

At first the narrator is her interpreter, and when
her own words are given, they only have FIS (free
indirect speech) form; we are thus made to feel
her modesty and shyness, for it seems that the
words have to be coaxed out of her. Even when
she speaks up, she sems hardly able to look at
Edmund, and can hardly arrogate the self-assertive
"I" for herself. And as from this point on the
conversation then proceeds in direct speech on
both sides... we actually experience her growth of
confidence and trust in the very form of the dialogue.

Edmund himself, who is far from perceptive, never

* Numbers after quotations refer to the chapters from which the
quotations are taken.

notices Fanny's growing passion for him and she of course represses it. In these circumstances, says John Wiltshire, her "desire, unable to be communicated in words, is expressed, experienced within and displayed covertly by the body".

It is jealousy which prompts the first sign of this desire. Wanting to give Mary Crawford a riding lesson, Edmund borrows the mare he has given to Fanny. Fanny, who is used to being neglected, is then nagged out of the house by her Aunt Norris and, looking across the park, sees the lesson in progress.

Edmund and Miss Crawford both on horseback, riding side by side, Dr and Mrs Grant, and Mr Crawford, with two or three grooms, standing about and looking on. A happy party it appeared to her – all interested in one object – cheerful beyond a doubt, for the sound of merriment ascended even to her. It was a sound that did not make her cheerful; she wondered that Edmund should forget her, and felt a pang. She could not turn her eyes from the meadow, she could not help watching all that passed. At first Miss Crawford and her companion made a circuit of the field, which was not small, at a foot's pace; then at her apparent suggestion, they rose to a canter; and to Fanny's timid nature it was astonishing to see how well she sat. After a few minutes, they stopt entirely, Edmund was close to her, he was speaking to her, he was evidently directing her management of the bridle, he had hold

of her hand; she saw it, or the imagination supplied
what the eye could not reach. She must not wonder
at this; what could be more natural than that
Edmund should be making himself useful, and
proving his good nature by any one? (7)

This famous scene is evidence enough that Fanny is
not the detached observer some critics hold her to
be. As Fanny watches Edmund and Mary together,
we feel her increasingly aroused jealousy. "After a
few minutes, they stopt entirely, Edmund was close
to her..." John Wiltshire points out that a full stop
might be expected after "entirely". Instead we have
a comma – Fanny's excitement does not "stop
entirely":

> the five observations included in the sentence
> progressively build up, as it accelerates with the
> increasing intimacy of the gestures she strains to
> catch sight of. 'She saw it': the sentence's climax
> encloses Fanny's excitement at the same time as
> it mimics the gesture – Edmund enclosing Mary's
> hand – that is its provocation.

Yet Fanny can't quite see: the word "reach" is brilliantly chosen, suggesting her straining imagination as she tries to take in the scene. It is as if she is
actually willing it to happen, says Jane Stabler in
her introduction to the Penguin *Mansfield Park*.
Much later, she shows the "same perversity" when
she wishes Edmund would stop deferring his

proposal of marriage to Mary:

> *"There is no good in this delay," said she. "Why is it not settled?... Oh! write, write. Finish it at once. Let there be an end to this suspense." (13)*

By making Fanny desire the very thing she dreads most, just to be free of the suspense, says Stabler, Austen

> shows a shrewd understanding of the workings of sexual jealousy as her heroine participates vicariously in the progress of the other relationship and almost yearns for the evidence that will confirm her worst suspicions.

While watching the riding lesson, she immediately tries to suppress the jealousy she feels – "what could be more natural than that Edmund should be making himself useful...?" Highly agitated, she pretends to herself that she feels pity for the horse being ridden too vigorously, and walks towards Edmund and Mary "with a great anxiety" to appear calm and gracious. The whole passage thus manages to show both the intensity of Fanny's desire and the energy she devotes to repressing it. The mixture of loneliness and envy she feels is caught in the sentence: "The sound of merriment ascended even to her." Her geographical separation from the group reflects her emotional isolation.

Passages like this count for little among Fanny's

harshest detractors, who, over the years, have written her off as "a human sea anemone" (an anonymous critic), "a frozen block of timidity" (Martin Mudrick), "a penniless dull little nobody" (Reginald Farrer), "a dreary, debilitated, priggish goody-goody" (D.W. Harding), and much else besides. Writing in the 1990s, Sandra Gilbert and Susan Gubar talk of her "invalid passivity" and argue that as a model of domestic virtue – "dependent, helpless, friendless, neglected, forgotten" – she resembles Snow White not only in her passivity but in her invalid deathliness, her immobility, her pale purity". To Marilyn Butler, Fanny's "feebleness" is merely a failed "device" for securing the reader's sympathy.

But it is plainly wrong to see Fanny merely as a silent, meek little weakling. She is not afraid to say what she thinks, giving her views on all kinds of subjects, from the theatricals to the tradition of family worship. Several times she tells Edmund: "I cannot see things as you do." Her inner conflict is constant. After her ordeal cutting roses we are told she had been "struggling against discontent and envy for some days"; during the theatricals she is "full of jealousy and agitation"; later, she feels Edmund's praise of her as a "stab".

If you "obliterate" Fanny's desire, as many critics do, says John Wiltshire, you cannot understand her invalidism, "which is her desire, thwarted and concealed, expressing itself through her body". It is true that Fanny is often represented as tired, and "trembling", but this can be explained (at least partly) by the stress she feels but can never show. The headaches, weariness and trembling are "bodily manifestations" of her "besieged" condition, as are her constant blushes, "another symptom conjoining desire and powerlessness". Fanny blushes more than 20 times during the novel, a constant reminder to the reader both of the intensity of her emotions and of her need to conceal them.

> Her pure, and eloquent blood
> Spoke in her cheeks, and so distinctly wrought
> That one might almost say, her body thought...

wrote John Donne. Fanny's blood is eloquent, too. Blushes are involuntary, and hard as she tries to control her mind, she can't always control her body.

Fanny is certainly "the most blushful" of Austen's heroines, says another sympathetic modern critic, John Mullan, in *What Matters in Jane Austen?* She "colours" in righteousness in response to some of the Crawfords' thoughtless jests. When Edmund talks to Fanny about his feelings for Mary Crawford, she asks him not to confide in her. "The time may come," she says, thinking of their possible marriage, and breaking off. "The colour rushed into her cheeks as she spoke." Edmund, as so often, fails to understand her response. He think she is "being delicate", says Mullan. "In fact her rush of blood tells us of her pained consciousness that her own love for him is doomed – and that she is entirely oblivious of it."

Much later, after Henry Crawford has proposed, and Fanny said no, Mary wonders playfully about her apparent "indifference" and asks whether "'you are so insensible as you profess yourself'... There was indeed so deep a blush over Fanny's face at that moment, as might warrant strong suspicion in a pre-disposed mind." But Fanny is not in the least "insensible"; Mary, like everyone else, is deluded about her. Fanny, says Mullan, "blushes because she is a virtuous girl who finds all this talk of love mortifying – but also because love does govern her every thought".

The extent of Fanny's feelings becomes evident at the moment when we learn of Maria and Henry's adultery. Edmund tells Fanny about it, and about Mary's inadequate response to it – she showed "no reluctance, no horror, no feminine... no modest loathings". On hearing this, Fanny, contemplating everyone's miseries, finds "she was in the greatest danger of being exquisitely happy". In this, says Janet Todd, she foreshadows Anne Elliot, the heroine of Austen's last novel, *Persuasion*, who revels in the moment when her rival's moral inferiority finally becomes apparent to the hero.

This response is very different from the Johnsonian sounding "consciousness of being born to struggle and endure", which the contrite Sir Thomas takes as her exemplary message. Rather, it displays "the enthusiasm of a woman's love", in keeping with the secret fetishising of the scrap of

Edmund's letter bearing the conventional "My very dear Fanny".

The early critic Richard Whately's verdict – so different to that of so many of his successors – that Fanny's passion "tinges" all her thoughts and actions is endorsed by Todd. "The men, Edmund and Henry, abandon their love when they find obstacles – Fanny retains her hungry love whatever seems in its way."

How much should we like the Crawfords?

The different ways of life in London and rural Mansfield, and the different influence each exerts, are constantly touched on in the novel. In Tony Tanner's view, Mansfield, "at its best, perfects people, London, at its worst perverts them". It is in London that Maria falls into the ways which lead to her adultery and ultimate disgrace, that Julia involves herself with the worthless Mr Yates, that Tom becomes unhappy and nearly loses his life. Above all, it is London "which has made and formed the attractive Crawfords, who very nearly bring total ruin to the world of Mansfield Park".

The Crawfords, in Tanner's view, are not villains; they have "many of the most superficially attractive qualities". But they have been "spoilt and subtly corrupted by their prolonged immersion in the amoral fashionable world". (It was, it is worth remembering, the age of Beau Brummell.) Fanny, we read, "was disposed to think the influence of London very much at war with all respectable attachments". And so it proves: it is a world of glamour and and excitement, but it is also a world, says Tanner, "in which manners substitute for morals, a world given over to cold deception, manipulation and exploitation".

The critic and psychologist D.W. Harding takes a more indulgent view. "We go badly astray if we think of [the Crawfords] simply as the representatives of the trivial metropolitan code," he says. Mary is cynical ("I look upon the Frasers to be about as unhappy as most other married people") and at times behaves inexcusably. But she is capable of a "natural warmth of heart" and "decency of feeling". Worldly Henry and Mary may be, but, in a novel where sibling relationships prove to be stronger than marital ones, they are always kind and loving to one another, and can be seen to exemplify the brother and sister tie shown to be so important in the relationship between William and Fanny.

Mansfield Park is deeply interested in how childhood shapes us, and the backgrounds of Mary and Fanny mirror one other. Both are vulnerable and insecure, separated from their parents in childhood and growing up with uncles and aunts, each having to come to terms with an adoptive home and find a way of coping. Fanny, under

Edmund's influence, armours herself with a sternly moral outlook, Mary copes by adopting more or less the opposite. But Mary's adoptive home has been very different to Fanny's, her uncle, Admiral Crawford, being a "man of vicious conduct" who, on his wife's death, "chose... to bring his mistress under his own roof" (4). She is witty and cynical – "of Rears and Vices, I saw enough," she crudely jokes to the solemn Edmund – but her cynicism hints at a damaged life. When she is married, she tells Mrs Grant, she will be a staunch defender of the marriage state, adding: "I wish my friends would be too. It would save me many a heartache." Her brother later tells her he won't consult his uncle about his plans to marry Fanny. "The Admiral hated marriage, and thought it never pardonable in a young man of independent fortune."

There are good reasons to sympathise with the Crawfords, but, as we quickly see, they are unscrupulous and manipulative. In a sense, says John Mullan, this is a novel about its heroine's absence – most of the crucial decisions which affect Fanny's life are made when she isn't there. Witness "the number of exchanges that take place without her".

It is often claimed that Austen never wrote scenes featuring only men – and there is only one such a scene in *Pride and Prejudice* (a short report of a conversation between Mr Bingley and Mr Bennet). But there are several in *Mansfield Park*. On his return from Antigua, Sir Thomas meets Mr

Yates rehearsing speeches in the billiard room; in the next chapter, Edmund talks to his father, exonerating Fanny from any role in the theatricals; later, the two men twice discuss Henry Crawford's proposal of marriage and how to persuade Fanny to accept it.

Austen gives us "these accumulated glimpses of men together as if respecting the Bertrams' aristocratic delusion that all important decisions are made by father and son", says Mullan. But much more important is the sequence of five conversations at the Parsonage among the Crawfords and Mrs Grant. These conversations show where the real "power" lies in the novel. Cumulatively, they are "the most shocking exchanges in all Austen's fiction".

The first occurs before the Crawfords even meet the Bertrams. Mrs Grant, however, already has plans. "Henry, you shall marry the youngest Miss Bertram," she says. Henry bows and thanks her. Mary warns her sister she is wasting her efforts. "He is the most horrible flirt that can be imagined. If your Miss Bertrams do not like to have their hearts broke, let them avoid Henry." As Mullan says, it is a pretty accurate prediction of what is to come. Henry quotes Milton's *Paradise Lost*, with a mischievous emphasis. "I consider the blessing of a a wife as most justly described in those discreet lines of the poet – 'Heaven's last best gift.'" Mary says: "There, Mrs Grant you see how he dwells on one word, and only look at his smile. I assure you he is very detestable; the Admiral's lessons have quite spoiled him." There is something chilling in this joking between brother and sister, Mary's mock-condemnatory "horrible" and "detestable" measuring, in Mullan's phrase, "the distance from any real disapproval of [Henry's] habitual behaviour".

The effect of these conversations at the Parsonage is to make the Bertrams and Fanny "seem unconscious players in the Crawfords' amusing game". In the second, Mary asks Henry if he really prefers Julia, given that Maria is "generally thought the handsomest". The jesting, says Mullan, is becoming dangerous: it is clear now that Maria will be Henry's likely prey – it is obvious she doesn't care "three straws" for Mr Rushworth, says Mary. During the preparations for the play, there is a conversation between Mary and Mrs Grant, with Mary again showing her scorn for Mr Rushworth.

"I would not give much for Mr Rushworth's chance if Henry stept in before the articles were signed."

(16)

Mary is speaking to her sister with cold candour: she sees that Henry has attracted both the Bertram girls, and she speaks as if he has done this kind of thing before. As Mullan says: "If only [Fanny] or the Bertrams could hear this! Fanny has observed Henry's flirtations with alarm, but her suspicions hardly go far enough."

Even more chilling is the next Parsonage conversation, between Henry and Mary alone. "Seeing the coast clear of the rest of the family", he asks his sister with a smile: "And how do you think I mean to amuse myself, Mary, on the days that I do not hunt?... my plan is to make Fanny Price in love with me" (24). Mary's reply is hardly good-hearted. "Fanny Price! Nonsense! No, no. You ought to be satisfied with her two cousins." To which her brother's rejoinder is devilish. "But I cannot be satisfied without Fanny Price, without making a small hole in Fanny Price's heart." Don't make her "really unhappy", says Mary. He has only a fortnight, so "will not do her any harm". He wants only to make her feel, when he leaves, "that she will be never happy again". "Moderation itself!" says Mary.

Fanny's presence, however, proves to be more alluring than Henry bargains for and in the final Parsonage conversation he tells Mary his plans have changed and he is determined to marry her. "Lucky, lucky girl!" exclaims his sister, assuming she will naturally comply. As ever, Fanny's fate is being decided while she isn't there.

"The fact is that most readers love the Crawfords, which is why some critics have to work with such nit-picking assiduity to find, or even create, retrospective faults in them," writes the contemporary critic, Roger Gard, in an often persuasive essay on the novel. Mary's saucy wit may be one reason; her love for her brother another; her blunders, too, may help explain why readers prefer her to the heroine. (She is always wrong about Fanny and we "like people who make mistakes", says John Mullan.) But it is hardly nit-picking, or especially hard work, to look carefully at the five scenes in the Parsonage, as Mullan has done, and to acknowledge that their cumulative effect should put us on our guard about Henry and Mary, however "loveable" we may find them. *

* John Mullan points out that Austen knew men like this. In 1801 she wote of her sister-in-law Eliza finding the manners of Lord Craven "very pleasing indeed", before adding: "The little flaw of having a Mistress now living with him at Ashdown Park, seems to be the only unpleasing circumstance about him."

What is the significance of the trip to Sotherton?

Mansfield Park is changed utterly by the arrival of the Crawfords: Maria, Julia, Edmund and Fanny are all unsettled by it and the sudden awakening of desire it triggers. Just as the scene-painter in the theatricals makes five of the housemaids "dissatisfied", so the arrival of Henry and Mary has a similar effect upstairs. Both Bertram sisters fall for Henry, while Edmund is captivated by Mary, and Fanny, as we have seen, looks on mute and jealous.

Maria, however – considering her future and longing to escape Mansfield – feels she has a "moral obligation" to marry the witless Mr Rushworth, with his country estate and London townhouse, and shortly after they become engaged, the party decide to visit Mr Rushworth's estate, Sotherton Court, with a view to examining what "improvements" can be made to it.

The outing to Sotherton has been called one of the great dramatic achievements of Austen's fiction. It is a "powerful and troubling" sequence, says Janet Todd, with Austen using it, in an experimentally symbolic way, to explore the "complex interaction" between the inner and outer lives of her characters and the true nature of their desires. Fanny is not the only one to feel sexual anguish in *Mansfield Park*; Maria feels it too, and when the journey to Sotherton begins, and she is forced to sit inside the carriage while her sister, Julia, sits with Henry in front, she is miserable:

> *For the first seven miles Maria had very little real comfort; her prospect always ended in Mr Crawford and her sister sitting side by side full of conversation and merriment; and to see only his expressive profile as he turned with a smile to Julia, or to catch the laugh of the other, was a perpetual source of irritation, which her own sense of propriety could but just smooth over. (8)*

Inwardly seething with jealousy, Maria strains to keep her social poise. Later, both Bertram sisters manoeuvre to get as close as possible to Henry and as far away as possible from Mr Rushworth and, in Julia's words, "his horrible mother" and "my tiresome aunt". "Austen's choreography throughout the Sotherton visit is a brilliant piece of prose stagecraft in which a large group of characters divides and re-merges into couples, isolated individuals, or other groups," says Jane Stabler.

As they all gather in the modernised chapel, Julia calls Henry's attention to her sister, saying "Do look at Mr Rushworth and Maria, standing side by side, exactly as if the ceremony were going to be performed" – intending, of course, to draw attention to the fact that while Maria is engaged she, Julia, is free. But the gambit backfires: Henry's competitive instincts are aroused and "stepping forward to Maria, [he] said, in a voice which she only could hear, 'I do not like to see Miss Bertram so near the altar.'" Maria, we are told, "instinctively moved a step or two, but recovering herself in a moment, affected to laugh". With Maria standing between Rushworth, her husband-to-be, and Henry, her adulterous lover-to-be, she pretends to be in control of the situation but the scene reflects her uncertainty and in so doing foreshadows her sexual crime at the end of the novel.

In a different part of the chapel, the exchange between Mary, Edmund and Fanny also forecasts the future. Mary, told that the family habit of gathering for morning and evening prayers has been discontinued, jokes that "Every generation has its improvements", which provokes Fanny into an unusually long speech defending the custom. Mary, however, continues the attack and Fanny angrily waits for Edmund to rebuke her. Instead Edmund merely contrasts her "lively mind" with the seriousness of the subject. But then Mary, too, is thrown; having scorned the clergy – "A clergyman is nothing" – she suddenly learns that Edmund himself intends to be ordained. We see her "rallying her spirits, and recovering her complexion", but the same kind of self-indulgent frivolity will lead to her ultimate rejection by Edmund.

All has gone awry in the chapel, and the party leaves it to find what the narrator calls "happy independence" and to indulge in "fault-finding", theoretically of the park though also, as it turns out, of each other. The layout of the garden is significant.

First there is a walled lawn, where nature is tamed and civilised, then the group move beyond that to a "wilderness" which is really a wood, but darker and less domesticated than the lawn. The wood "is a version of the Renaissance topos of the wood of love – la selva d'amore", says Tony Tanner, "always understood as a dark maze in which one loses one's way". It is here that Mary tries to undermine Edmund's intention to be a clergyman and in the course of their conversation they leave "the great path" and take "a very serpentine course" – outer action once again mimicking the life within.

It is here, too, that Fanny says she is tired. Mary says she isn't, mischievously combating Edmund's sense of distance and time with her "feminine lawlessness". Excited by Mary's proximity, Edmund abandons his cousin for the walk. All save Fanny, now seated because tired, stray beyond the ordered "wilderness" – in reality no more than a part of the garden planted with trees – into the wilder park, its wildness, perhaps, suggestive of the errors of judgement they will later make. Mary and Edmund go through an unlocked entrance but Maria and Henry face a barrier, a locked iron gate in the ha-ha.

The park beyond the wilderness draws on a long literary tradition of dangerous wild places, in Spenser and Shakespeare and Milton's *Paradise Lost*, as well as in Samuel Richardson's novel, *Clarissa*, where the heroine is tricked through a gate into her seducer's power and her own ruin.

The locked gates may also be a reference to virginity, just as in medieval paintings a locked garden often represented virginity. Maria, says Janet Todd, "has for the first time felt desire and is desperate to escape Mansfield Park through Henry rather than her dull fiancé". Henry begins:

> "You have a very smiling scene before you."
>
> "Do you mean literally or figuratively? Literally, I conclude. Yes, certainly the sun shines, and the park looks very cheerful. But unluckily that iron gate, that ha-ha, give me a feeling of restraint and hardship. 'I cannot get out,' as the starling said." As she spoke, and it was with expression, she walked to the gate; he followed her. "Mr Rushworth is so long fetching the key!"
>
> "And for the world you would not get out without the key and without Mr Rushworth's authority and protection, or I think you might with little difficulty pass round the edge of the gate, here, with my assistance; I think it might be done, if you really wished to be more at large, and could allow yourself not to be prohibited."
>
> "Prohibited! nonsense! I certainly can get out that way, and I will..." (10)

The allusion in which Maria voices her frustration – "I cannot get out, as the starling said" – refers to an incident in Laurence Stern's *A Sentimental Journey Through France and Italy* (1768), where a caged bird provides Yorick, the sentimental traveller, with an image of his own condition – he has been threatened with imprisonment in the Bastille. The episode shows how vulnerable Maria is. She is only half-aware of what she is about. Kathryn Sutherland writes:

> A fortune hunter, playing the game she thinks she understands and for which she has been trained from birth by education and her father's social anxiety, what she does not take into account is the strength of her own passions.

Both Edmund and Sir Thomas also badly underestimate her capacity for feeling ("her feelings are not strong," Edmund tells Fanny (7)). In her passion, she is reminiscent of Mary Wollstonecraft's turbulent heroine, Maria, who "wished to be only alive for love" but whom "marriage had bastilled". Part of the design of this "designing novel", says Sutherland, is that the social and moral fortunes of Fanny Price and Maria Bertram reverse the economic trajectories of their namesake mothers. Indeed, the fates of the younger Fanny and Maria are explicit in their mutual criticism and in the statement they together make about the role of women in the moral economy of the family: where Fanny compensates for her propertyless status in acts of strict propriety, Maria abandons property for impropriety.

In a quiet way, Sutherland suggests, *Mansfield Park* rehearses the temptation and fall sequences of *Paradise Lost*: Maria in her sexual fall, like Mary in her "feminine lawlessness", plays the old Eve against Fanny's reformed Eve. Only Fanny refuses to stray from the garden at Sotherton; only Fanny does not succumb to Henry Crawford's temptations.

It all ends in confusion. Mr Rushworth appears, upset he has been left behind; Julia arrives, breathless and angry. When everyone meets again, says Tanner, "one feels that some irreparable damage has been done... Nothing constructive has been achieved, but the seeds of future disharmony have been sown..."

The journey home is equally disharmonious. While the women passengers, as Janet Todd puts it, are "mentally fatigued and erotically disappointed", tensions run high in Henry's barouche. When Mrs Norris, heaving with goodies she has sponged, demands, in her usual querulous mode, that Fanny show gratitude for the "indulgence" of a day out, Maria, for once, comes to her defence. She is motivated not by a sense of justice but, says Todd,

by her own unbounded materialism that prompts her to guard with a jealous eye even the pheasant's eggs of a man she would gladly jilt. To present with precision yet without apparent moral judgement the casual manifestations of human egotism is one of the great achievements of Austen's comedy in this novel.

Why do the theatricals matter?

The theatricals "provide the core of the book", says Tony Tanner. The passage dealing with them, he thinks, is "one of the most subtle and searching" in English fiction, Austen's treatment of them, and their relevance to modern life amply justifying the American critic Lionel Trilling's claim that "it was Jane Austen who first represented the specifically modern personality and the culture in which it had its being".

The decision to stage a play may seem harmless enough, especially as Austen's own family enjoyed acting themselves. But in the novel, suggests Tanner, Austen uses the theatricals to explore the implications of acting and role-playing for the individual and society. The attempt to turn Mansfield Park into a theatre is "a dangerous act of desecration: it is like transforming a temple of order into a school for scandal". All the characters sense that Sir Thomas would disapprove, but the real problem is a deeper one: acting (as Plato suggested) can have a debasing influence on the civilised self. Role-playing militates against stability: if the self is fluid, as acting suggests, there is no limit to what it might do. "Instead of life conceived as a rigid adherence to firm moral standards, it may turn into a series of improvisations suggested by the milieu of the moment, an endless metamorphosis."

Mansfield Park, says Tanner, is a place "where you must be true to your best self: the theatre is a place where you can explore and experiment with other selves. A person cannot live in both." Only Fanny, says Tanner, is responsibly clear-sighted enough to resist the impulse to take part, and while Tom overrules Edmund's objections by saying "His [Sir Thomas's] house shall not be hurt", Mansfield Park is all but destroyed by the theatricals, which set in train the series of events that culminate in Maria's disgrace and Julia's elopement.

Trilling's view, as often with this novel, is similar to Tanner's. He ascribes to Austen "a traditional, almost primitive feeling about dramatic imper-sonation... the fear that the impersonation of a bad or inferior character will have a harmful effect upon the impersonator; that, indeed, the impersonation of any other self will diminish the integrity of the real self". It is hard to find much textual evidence for this claim, interesting as it is. The objections to the theatricals are clearly stated by Edmund, and they are more practical.

"I think it would be very wrong. In a general light, private theatricals are open to some objections, but as we are circumstanced, I must think it would be highly judicious, and more than injudicious, to attempt anything of the kind. It would show great want of feeling on my father's account, absent as he is, and in some degree of constant danger; and it would be imprudent, I think, with regard to Maria,

whose situation is a very delicate one, considering
everything, extremely delicate." (13)

Edmund is referring here to Maria's unofficial engagement – and the play finally chosen, after a good deal of squabbling, does nothing to alleviate his objections: it is, he thinks, "exceedingly unfit for private representation". What Edmund fears, in short, is not so much the danger of acting in general, but the reason his sisters want to act, which is to further their intimacy with Henry. He has a point. The play selected is certain to lead to unease in a house already full of sexual tensions. "We are left in no doubt," says David Lodge, "that the would-be actors are not seriously interested in the play as an artistic production, but as an opportunity for a feast of Misrule, for showing off and bringing themselves into various piquant and intimate relationships."

Lovers' Vows, adapted by Elizabeth Inchbald from *Das Kind der Liebe* (*Child of Love*) by Kotzebue, and first performed in England in 1798, has a radical agenda even if it has a sentimental ending: a worldly baron who has seduced and then abandoned a chambermaid in his youth, wants to sell off his daughter, Amelia, to a rich lout. Amelia herself, however, has other ideas. She wants to marry the shy young clergyman, Anhalt. Fanny disapproves of both female roles – "the situation of one, and the language of the other, so unfit to be expressed by any woman of modesty". No wonder Fanny is disturbed, says the feminist critic Claudia

Johnson: an unwed single mother and a lively young woman in love with a shy young clergyman who has "formed" her mind both show women bold and independent enough to assert their sexuality.

In the original German version Amelia's declaration of love almost amounts to a proposal. Inchbald toned this down. Recognising that "the forward and unequivocal manner in which she [Amelia] announces her affection to her lover in the original would have been revolting to an English audience", Inchbald renders Amelia's declaration of love "by whimsical insinuations, rather than coarse abruptness". Enough indelicacy remains, however, to scandalise Fanny, says Johnson, "even as it discloses her own unenacted desires for the clergyman who has formed her mind". Austen gives further prominence to female desire (as expressed in the play) when Mary Crawford asks the bold question – "What gentleman among you am I to have the pleasure of making love to?" – and meets with stunned silence.

In the end it is Edmund who plays the clergyman Anhalt opposite Mary's Amelia. Fanny, though she refuses to act, knows the play almost by heart and is interested "most particularly" in the scene where Amelia "announces her affection": it is one "which she was longing and dreading to see how they would perform".

She had read, and read the scene again with many painful, many wondering emotions, and looked

forward to their representation of it as a
circumstance almost too interesting. (18)

Fanny's discomfort increases when Mary arrives in her East room to ask for help rehearsing; she is followed by Edmund with a similar request and, in the end, the two decide to do the scene with each other while Fanny acts as prompter. Anhalt (Edmund) is Amelia's tutor, whom she has grown to love; he has taught her everything, but is blind to the passion he has inspired – all this is clear from the dialogue. "My father has more than once told me that he who forms my mind I should always consider my greatest benefactor," says Amelia (Mary), coyly, "looking down": "My heart tells me the same." Since he has indeed formed her mind and gained her affections, Edmund's true partner in the scene should really be Fanny, not Mary. Fanny's almost obsessive interest in the scene, says John Wiltshire, can thus be readily explained,

> for it holds up a mirror to her, showing her relationship to Edmund, a mirror all the more fascinating to gaze into because only she can look at it, and because it is so distorted. Not only is the barrier to marriage Anhalt's rather than Amelia's poverty and dependence, but Amelia's coquettish effrontery is an unthinkably shameful reflection of Fanny's unspoken desires.

Poor Fanny is thus not only forced to be present

while Mary, under cover of the play, courts Edmund; she is forced to witness her rival act out her own forbidden, secret desire: it is hardly surprising she is overcome.

> *To prompt them must be enough for her; and it was sometimes more than enough; for she could not always pay attention to the book. In watching them she forgot herself; and agitated by the increasing spirit of Edmund's manner, had once closed the play and turned away exactly as he wanted help. It was imputed to very reasonable weariness, and she was thanked and pitied; but she deserved their pity, more than she hoped they would ever surmise. (18)*

On the surface, the objections to the theatricals involve propriety and decorum. But we are never in any doubt that what might be called the "moral destiny" of the characters is also at stake: while Tony Tanner, and others, believe Austen to be showing the dangers of pretending to be other people, the actual play becomes, in theological language, "a proximate occasion of sin". This is true not just of Mary, who is able to advance her relationship with Edmund under the guise of playing a part, but also of Maria who secures the part of Agatha, the abandoned mother, giving her the chance for closer contact with Henry, who plays Frederick, her illegitimate son.

Julia, who also wanted to play Agatha, is furious.

*The sister with whom she was used to be on easy
terms was now become her greatest enemy: they
were alienated from each other; and Julia was not
superior to the hope of some distressing end to the
attentions which were still carrying on there, some
punishment to Maria for conduct so shameful
towards herself as well as towards Mr Rushworth.*

(18)

This is another example of Austen's brilliant use of
free indirect speech. Here, says John Mullan, we
move from a description of Julia's unstated feelings
to something more indirect. The evasive phrase
"some distressing end" suggests Julia is hoping her
sister's behaviour will lead to scandal and disgrace,
while the sentence finishes with what Mullan calls
a whole-hearted adoption of what must be Julia's
own thought pattern, imagining Maria's punishment "for conduct so shameful towards herself as
well as towards Mr Rushworth". "Shameful" is not
the author's word, it is Julia's, as she pretends to
herself that she is exercising moral judgement
rather than feeling mere envy. We see Julia
convince herself that she is concerned about her
sister's conduct towards Mr Rushworth when all
she actually wants is Henry for herself. "Austen's
extraordinary narrative sophistication allows us
not just to know but somehow to experience Julia's
hypocrisy."

The stage directions of *Lovers' Vows* give ample
opportunity for Agatha and Frederick to embrace,

and the play intensifies the growing and dangerous physical intimacy between Maria and Henry. For example, one of Inchbald's stage directions in the first scene reads: "Frederick with his eyes cast down, takes her hand, and puts it to his heart." This is the scene being rehearsed when Julia arrives with the news that Sir Thomas has returned. Frederick is "listening with looks of devotion to Agatha's narrative, and pressing her hand to his heart..." Julia briefly suspends her jealousy but when she sees that "in spite of the shock of her words, he still kept his station and retained her sister's hand, her wounded heart swelled again with injury..."

Henry takes all the licence conservative critics detected in the original German drama, says Jane Stabler, while Maria's vain, provincial husband-to-be plays the vain, cosmopolitan Count Cassel. Rushworth's fussing about his "two and forty speeches" and his pink satin cloak makes him seem unmanly as well as stupid.

In Austen's novel and Inchbald's version of Kotzebue's play, masculine control is undercut on moral, sexual, and political fronts: Regency masculinity appears to be as much a part to be learned (and forgotten) as feminine decorum. When Sir Thomas finds himself face to face with the Honourable John Yates playing the discredited Baron Wildenhaim in his study, he confronts a version of his own hollow authority.

Having put an end to the theatricals, Sir Thomas concentrates on trying to remove "every outward memento of what had been". This attention to appearances is typical of him, but while he treats *Lovers' Vows* as a proscribed text, "burning all that met his eye", it is not the play itself which is at fault, says Stabler, "but what it reveals about the thwarted desires of its participants". And the desires and jealousies stirred up by the theatricals in *Mansfield Park* will not be so easily done away with.

Superficially, though, with Sir Thomas's return, the house returns to its former "sameness and gloom". Edmund eventually looks back at the theatricals as "that period of general folly". Mary, on the other hand, recalls them as her finest hour: "If I had the power of recalling any one week of my existence, it should be that week..." Henry also rejoices in the memory. "We were all alive... I never was happier." Tony Tanner says this reveals the truth about the Crawfords: "they only feel alive in acting a role... in repose, they are nothing". They can mimic all feelings because "deep down" they feel nothing. They are "doomed to be insincere" and in this, "in their strange combination of energy and emptiness they are a very modern pair".

Is Fanny right to resist Henry Crawford?

No sooner does Fanny escape one threat than she faces another. Henry's unwanted proposal of marriage comes quickly after the theatricals, and, for one so vain and lazy, he presses his suit with surprising energy: having decided to try and make Fanny fall in love with him – "It would be something to be loved by such a girl, to excite the first ardours of her young, unsophisticated mind!" – he, much to his own surprise and his sister's delight, falls in love with her.

To Claire Tomalin, this love is hard to credit. Fanny is

> cautious and censorious. Jokes make her and her cousin Edmund uneasy. She takes joy in the stars, in music and poetry and flowers, and in her brother, William; but she is not a joyous person, perhaps because her childhood experiences have dried up something in her spirit. Not only is she the least joyous of all Austen's heroines, she is the most reluctant to open her mouth; when she does she speaks in a stilted and wooden manner. This is credible, but it is one of the things that make it hard to believe that Henry Crawford could ever fall in love with her.

Tony Tanner thinks her saintly and unsexy, arguing that her marriage will be "perhaps the most nearly asexual marriage among the marriages achieved by Jane Austen's heroines". Roger Gard agrees she is unsexy ("for me, the perhaps is unnecessary"); nor is he persuaded by the feminist critic Margaret Kirkham's notion that "her apparent saintliness is closely connected with her ability to excite sexual passion".

The literary woodenness in Fanny's utterances is understandable given her sheltered background. The chapel at Sotherton fails to live up to Walter Scott, for example – "no aisles, no arches, no inscriptions, no banners..." – and there are Shakespearian echoes in her reaction to the August night when she looks out of the drawing room at Mansfield.

> *"Here's harmony!" said she, "Here's repose! Here's what may leave all painting and all music behind... Here's what may tranquillise every care, and lift the heart to rapture! When I look out on such a night as this, I feel as if there could be neither wickedness nor sorrow in the world..." (11)*

Edmund, at whom this is aimed, only remarks "I like to hear your enthusiasm, Fanny!" and soon allows himself to be drawn away from star-gazing by Mary, who is playing the piano, while Fanny herself is scolded away from the window by Mrs Norris. It is a good example of what Mary Lascelles calls "youth sympathetically observed" – a reminder that Fanny is indeed very young.

The chapter in which Henry tells Mary of his love shows the subtlety with which Austen handles the Crawfords. There is something touching about Mary's pleasure and Henry's enthusiasm.

*"Had you seen her this morning, Mary!" he
continued, "attending with such ineffable sweetness
and patience, to all the demands of her aunt's
stupidity, working with her, and for her, her colour
beautifully heightened as she leant over the work,
then returning to her seat to finish a note which she
was previously engaged in writing for that stupid
woman's service, and all this with such unpretending
gentleness, so much as a matter of course that she
was not to have a moment at her own command, her
hair arranged as neatly as it always is, and one little
curl falling forward as she wrote, which she now and
then shook back, and in the midst of this, still
speaking at intervals to me, or listening, and as if
she liked to listen to what I said. Had you seen her
so, Mary, you would not have implied the possibility
of her power over my heart ever ceasing." (30)*

This suggests Fanny's apparent saintliness is part
of her attraction. To Henry, says John Wiltshire,
Fanny "is a pre-Victorian Thackerian Amelia, bent
over her sewing, her sexual attractiveness
heightened by her weakness and innocence, and
the potential for mastery over it". In Henry's
fantasy, "as in all male fantasies of this kind", Fanny
is a "blank, or vacant space in which the desire,
once aroused, will be wholly directed at him".

Yet while Henry sees her as angelic and wants
to awaken in her the devotion she feels for her
brother, William (which he has witnessed), he is
also attracted by her courage. At the Grants' dinner

party, Henry talks about the theatricals, saying what a shame it was that Sir Thomas returned so soon.

> *...Fanny, averting her face, said with a firmer tone than usual, "As far as I am concerned, sir, I would not have delayed his return for a day. My uncle disapproved it all so entirely when he did arrive, that in my opinion, every thing had gone quite far enough."*
>
> *She had never spoken so much to him in her life before, and never so angrily to any one; and when her speech was over, she trembled and blushed at her own daring. (30)*

Typically, says Roger Gard, Fanny's self-assertion is couched in terms of disapproval, but "it is courageous, and therefore attractive. It is the key to what follows: Henry's falling in love."

The difficulty of winning Fanny's heart stirs Henry. He is determined to overcome her resistance; we always want what we can't have. But his true nature is clear to us, and comes out in the conversation with Mary. All women, he thinks, are fickle, and talking of Maria he says brutally: "I am not such a coxcomb as to suppose her feelings more lasting than other women's."

Just as Sir Thomas Bertram has clearly chosen his wife for her sex appeal, we "joltingly realize", says John Mullan, that Henry Crawford commits himself to marrying Fanny because of sexual longing. "'How the pleasing plague had stolen on him' he could not say." He knows he can only sleep with Fanny if he becomes her husband, and his sister later confirms both our sense of his yearning and of his ultimate fickleness when she says: "a wife you loved would be the happiest of women", adding that "even when you ceased to love, she would yet find in you the liberality and good-breeding of a gentleman" (30). Here, says Mullan, "as Austen expects the reader to notice, 'love' is synonymous with sexual appetite". Henry may not be able to acknowledge the possibility of "ceasing to love Fanny Price", but Mary can. She knows that her brother, if successful with Fanny, will eventually look elsewhere for his sexual pleasures.

Henry's shallowness is indicated by his skill as an actor: when he begins to read different speeches from *Henry VIII* Fanny is drawn to him despite herself: "she could not abstract her mind... she was forced to listen". It is apt that the play, which she chooses, should be one about a king famous for his struggle to decide whether to abandon his virtuous first wife for the charms of the vivacious "Anne Bullen".

Henry Crawford dabbles in acting as he dabbles in everything; at one stage he wonders about going into the navy, at another, he toys with the idea of becoming a responsible landowner. The determination he expresses in Portsmouth to show himself "master of my own property" is likely to be as transient as all his other enthusiasms, as the narrator suggests.

He had gone [to Norfolk], had done even more good
than he had foreseen... and was now able to
congratulate himself upon it, and to feel, that in
performing a duty, he had secured agreeable
recollections for his own mind... This was aimed,
and well aimed, at Fanny. It was pleasing to hear
him speak so properly; here, he had been acting as he
ought to do. (15)

This is typical Henry, congratulating himself, performing a duty, securing agreeable recollections. He is staging a drama for Fanny's benefit, as the choice of words makes clear. With Henry, nothing lasts: charming but insincere, he falls for Fanny but only in so far as he is capable of falling for her: the capacity for deep feeling and lasting commitment is not part of his nature.

How sympathetic a figure is Sir Thomas Bertram?

"Of all the fathers of Jane Austen's novels, Sir Thomas is the only one to whom admiration is given," says Lionel Trilling. Like so many judgements about *Mansfield Park* this is, at best, half-true, and to be fair to Trilling he quickly qualifies it. Austen's "masculine ideal", he says, is exemplified by husbands, by Darcy, Knightley and Wentworth, "in whom principle and duty consort with a ready and tender understanding". The fathers in *Pride and Prejudice, Emma* and *Persuasion,* by contrast, "lack principle and fortitude", and the father's faults in *Mansfield Park* are soon made abundantly clear:

> if he learns to cherish Fanny as the daughter of his heart, he betrays the daughters of his blood. Maria's sin and her sister Julia's bad disposition are blamed directly upon his lack of intelligence and sensibility.

In *Mansfield Park,* says Janet Todd, Austen presents the military and the Church as the two professions which can do most to support England at "a difficult and sapping time", the one defending it abroad, the other stiffening moral fibre at home. But the moral principles for which men were fighting when the novel was written are sadly lacking in most of the inhabitants of Mansfield Park, not least in Sir Thomas himself. He is compromised by his "presumed ownership" of slaves in Antigua, says Todd, but most of all by his "insidious arrogance, which allows him to treat his children as commodities".

The moral deficiency in Mansfield Park is evident from the first paragraph of the novel, in which Austen chronicles, in seven brilliant sentences, the marriages of the three middle-class Ward sisters, making it clear that, in two cases, the alliance is based on money and social position –

one sister responding to an advantageous offer, the other a "not contemptible" one. The youngest marries a lowly lieutenant of marines, presumably for love and no money, thus cutting herself off from her family.

At Mansfield, much depends on Sir Thomas, whose wife is probably the silliest woman in all Jane Austen – what the 18th century feminist writer Mary Wollstonecraft would call "a vain inconsiderate doll". This hardly suggests good judgement, nor does his foolish encouragement of his daughter Maria to marry the inane Mr Rushworth.

Sir Thomas's fallibility is clear from the beginning. The story is set in motion by Tom's thoughtless extravagance, which has driven the family into debt and enraged his father.

> *"I blush for you, Tom," said he, in his most dignified manner. "I blush for the expedient which I am driven on, and I trust I may pity your feelings as a brother on the occasion. You have robbed Edmund for ten, twenty, thirty years, perhaps for life, of more than half the income which ought to be his." (3)*

But Sir Thomas blushes in vain. His children may be in awe of him, but they don't do what he wants. He may behave with dignity and decorum, but he has no real control over what goes on. The conservative notion of "parental authority", held up as an ideal by the philosopher Edmund Burke, is shown to fail in this novel. Sir Thomas's gravity, as Claudia Johnson puts it, "operates only as an external check, not as an internal inhibition..." His children "tremble at the detection, rather than the commission, of wrongs". We quickly learn that he is in the dark about the dispositions of his daughters, and that this is because of his own forbidding airs.

> *Sir Thomas did not know what was wanting, because, though a truly anxious father, he was not outwardly affectionate, and the reserve of his manner repressed all the flow of their spirits before him. (2)*

The dutifulness Sir Thomas assumes he has secured is thus a delusion. His dignity is undercut by his ignorance. Meanwhile, his wife sits on her sofa, quietly dozing, "a picture of health, wealth, ease and tranquility". Serene and vacuous, she is unconcerned about her children and oblivious of the intrigues they carry on under her nose. Johnson writes:

> Clearly the Burkean models of parental authority go awry in *Mansfield Park*. Dread of the potent father and fond concern for the delicate mother are just as likely to conceal or promote wrongdoing as they are to foster the capacity for generous feeling which in Austen's novels is possessed only by moral people.

Sir Thomas is anxious to think himself a good father, to satisfy himself as well as others of his "paternal judiciousness". But it is all a charade. He plainly sees that Maria despises Rushworth, but his offer to call off a marriage "so unquestionably advantageous" – one which would form "a connection exactly of the right sort; in the same country, and the same interest" – is half-hearted at best, disingenuous at worst. Sir Thomas should be candid with Maria but he isn't. When she assures him she does want to marry Rushworth, he is "too glad to be satisfied perhaps to urge the matter quite so far as his judgement might have dictated to others. It was an alliance which he could not have relinquished without pain" (21). He doesn't understand that she feels things deeply, that her only aim in marrying Rushworth is to escape Mansfield and him. When Elizabeth Bennet talks to her father in *Pride and Prejudice*, their relationship is one of mutual trust – he urges her not to marry without affection. This kind of trust is entirely missing in the relationship between Sir Thomas and his daughters.

But while Maria's status as a daughter entitles her to at least the appearance of choice, Fanny, as an indigent niece, is granted no such consideration. From Fanny, for all his shows of kindness, he expects obedience. When he "advises" her to retire to bed after the ball, the narrator makes clear that this is more than advice. "'Advise' was his word, but it was the advice of absolute power." In sending her away, we are told, he might be thinking merely of her health; "or he might mean to recommend her as a wife by shewing her persuadableness".

It is shortly after this that Sir Thomas talks to Fanny about Henry Crawford's offer. He expects her cheerfully to be guided by him and is amazed by her defiance, believing, absurdly, that she has been infected by pernicious radical doctrines.

> *"I had thought you peculiarly free from wilfulness of temper, self-conceit, and every tendency to that independence of spirit, which prevails so much in modern days, even in young women, and which in young women is offensive and disgusting beyond all common offence. But you have now shown me that you can be wilful and perverse, that you will decide for yourself, without any consideration or deference for those who have surely some right to guide you – without even asking your advice." (32)*

It is symptomatic of Sir Thomas's "breathtaking impercipience", says Johnson, that he attributes a radical agenda and ungovernable passion to the dutiful and mild-mannered Fanny. His interview with her mirrors the interview with Maria: "just as he attributes Maria's wish to marry a man she does not love to a commendable, because easily governable, serenity of temper, so he attributes Fanny's refusal to marry a man she does not love to a "young, heated fancy' and a 'wild fit of folly'..."

Fanny's hope that "to a man like her uncle, so

discerning, so honourable, so good, the simple acknowledgement of settled dislike on her side would have been sufficient" to end Henry's suit is a vain hope. Sir Thomas, indeed, behaves as if her "settled dislike" doesn't matter in the least. But then he is not a man, as Fanny herself later reflects, who worries about girls marrying undeserving husbands. "He who had married a daughter to Mr Rushworth. Romantic delicacy was certainly not to be expected from him." Nor does she win any sympathy from Edmund who, oblivious of her love for him, similarly tries to persuade her to marry Henry, suggesting she should feel thankful for the proposal and anxious not to disappoint such a worthy suitor. Here, as Johnson says, Fanny rankles in the manner of Elizabeth Bennet when the ridiculous Mr Collins proposes to her: surely, Fanny feels, "it ought not to be set down as certain, that a man must be acceptable to every woman he may happen to like himself".

But Fanny goes further than this, questioning the position she is put in as a modest girl: first, it seems, she is required to feel no desire at all, then she is expected to feel desire on demand. "How then was I to be – to be in love with him the moment he said he was with me? How was I to have an attachment at his service, as soon as it was asked for?"

There is no adequate way to answer Fanny's questions, says Johnson, for the "paradox of female purity" is not simply that the same purity which is supposed to place women above the suspicion of sexual desire actually inflames male desire. It is also that female purity itself is simultaneously demanded as natural and disbelieved as affected. From the outside, Fanny's refusal of Henry looks like the coquettish "no" Mr Collins has learned to expect from "elegant" females before hearing their inevitable, graceful "yes" – in short, like another of the many acts people in *Mansfield Park* stage for propriety's sake.

Fanny, in other words, becomes a victim of the very diffidence and gentleness she has been brought up to feel. And when, instead of being gratefully submissive to Sir Thomas, she bravely refuses to bow to his wishes, she is accused of exhibiting "independence of spirit" and "perverse" and "disgusting" desires. Nor does Henry give up. As she finds to her dismay, her "incurably gentle manner" only encourages him.

> *Her diffidence, gratitude, and softness, made every expression of indifference seem almost an effort of self-denial; seem, at least, to be giving nearly as much pain to herself as to him. (33)*

TEN FACTS
ABOUT *MANSFIELD PARK*

1.

The 1999 film adaptation of *Mansfield Park* broke from the original plot by including biographical details of Jane Austen's life. In it, the stories that Fanny Price writes are actually from Austen's *Juvenilia*, which were written when the author was a teenager.

2.

Though Austen's work is full of a sense of the precariousness of life, death itself features little. The only two people to die are Dr Grant in *Mansfield Park* and Mrs Churchill in *Emma*.

3.

Like all the novels Austen wrote during her lifetime *Mansfield Park* was originally published anonymously. The first edition of the book credits it to "the Author of *'Sense & Sensibility,'* and *'Pride & Prejudice.'"*

4.
Mansfield Park was the only book Austen wrote that received no reviews on its publication. But there was very little immediate criticism of any of her novels. Two reviews were published of *Sense and Sensibility*, three of *Pride and Prejudice* and seven of *Emma*.

5.
Mansfield Park was the first novel written by Austen entirely in her adult life. *Sense and Sensibility* and *Pride and Prejudice* were both revisions of works first drafted when she was younger.

6.
Mansfield Park is not, as commonly thought, an old English country house. Rather, it's a newly built mansion, possibly constructed on the proceeds of the slave trade. Any literate person at the time knew of England's famous Lord Chief Justice, Lord Mansfield, and his contribution to the abolition of the slave trade. It was also generally known that Mansfield had adopted his mixed-race great-niece, Dido Belle, to whom he was devoted.

7.
Whilst it is said in the novel that Maria Bertram is sent off to another country to live out a life of shame, she probably did not in fact travel abroad. At the time, people often spoke of other parts of the same country as "another country": Maria Bertram

and Mrs. Norris probably just moved to another part of the English countryside.

8.

Many recent films have made use of the plots of Austen novels, resetting them in the contemporary world. In Martin Scorsese's *Goodfellas* (1990), the plot of *Mansfield Park* is employed but with a surprising element of violence thrown in. Scorsese thought the violence appropriate, asserting that "there's an underlying violence in every word Austen wrote".

9.

The Hogwarts caretaker's cat in J.K. Rowling's *Harry Potter* series was named "Mrs. Norris" after the character in *Mansfield Park*.

10.

Mansfield Park might well be the first novel ever to depict the life of a young girl from her own perspective. Fanny is just 10 years old when she is taken from her loving Portsmouth home and shipped off to Mansfield Park.

Fanny was obliged to introduce him.

Why is Mrs Norris so unpleasant?

Mrs Norris is the most odious character in Jane Austen's fiction. Mean, spiteful and officious, she bullies those over whom she has power and sets out to make Fanny's life a misery. What is less often acknowledged is that her ability to do this is the direct result of Sir Thomas's mismanagement of his household and of his wife's complacency and indolence.

In eight years of having Fanny under her roof, the only advice Lady Bertram offers her is after Henry's proposal: "it is every woman's duty to accept such a very unexceptionable offer," she says. Virtually an imbecile, she takes an interest (if that is not too strong a word) only in her pug and her "work", meaning needlework, much of which seems to be done by Fanny. She barely notices her children and hardly seems to miss her husband when he is away. She sends her maid to help Fanny dress for the ball, too late to be of any use, and is happy to take credit for the result. Her generosity, says Claire Tomalin, "extends to giving her nephew William £10 but not to noticing how Fanny is ill-treated under her own roof".

"One of the most disturbing insights of the novel is to show how casually and unintentionally, members of a family are able to condone an abusive relationship within it," says Jane Stabler in her introduction to the Oxford edition. Thus we see not just how Aunt Norris's hostility to Fanny colours her whole existence, but also how members of the Bertram family effectively condone it. Even Edmund offers only rare, muted criticism of his aunt, appearing not to notice Fanny's suffering and making no objection when it is suggested that she leave Mansfield Park and go and live with her aunt.

Mrs Norris, says Tomalin, "is the sort of woman who feels herself strengthened and confirmed in her own position by the sufferings of others". Her spiteful attitude to Fanny, as Austen shrewdly notes, feeds on itself: "she disliked Fanny because she had neglected her". She enjoys, too, the discomfort of servants, implying that Sir Thomas is over-indulgent when he keeps his labourers on during the winter months, hearing with pleasure that two maids have been turned away at Sotherton "for wearing white gowns", and preventing one of the estate boys from being given the lunch he expects in the kitchen at Mansfield. Her behaviour would have been understood by Dr Johnson, a writer Austen hugely admired and who once wrote: "When female minds are imbittered by age or solitude, their malignity is generally exerted in a rigorous and spiteful superintendence of domestic trifles."

To Sir Thomas, Mrs Norris is both sycophantic and deceitful. Thrown by his displeasure about the theatricals when he returns from Antigua – a pastime which she encouraged – she turns the subject to her own efforts to further the connection with the Rushworth family. In organising a preliminary visit to Sotherton by Lady Bertram, she is full of her own praise, and, under the guise of sympathy for the coachman, of the huge sacrifice she has been prepared to make on his, Sir Thomas's, behalf:

"My dear Sir Thomas, if you had seen the state of the roads that day! I thought we should never have got through them, though we had four horses of course; and poor old coachman would attend us, out of his great love and kindness, though he was hardly able to sit the box on account of his rheumatism which I had been doctoring him for, ever since Michaelmas, I cured him at last; but he was very bad all the winter – and this was such a day, I could not help going up in his room before we set off to advise him not to venture: he was putting on his wig – so I said, 'Coachman, you had much better not go, your Lady and I shall be very safe; you know how steady Stephen is, and Charles has been upon the leaders so often now, that I am sure there is no fear. But, however, I soon found it would not do; he was bent upon going, and as I hate to be worrying and officious, I said no more; but my heart quite ached for him at every jolt, and when we got into the rough lanes about Stoke, where what with the frost and snow upon beds of stones, it was worse than any thing you can imagine, I was quite in agony about him. And then the poor horses too! – to see them

straining away! You know how I always feel for the
horses. And we got to the bottom of Sandcroft Hill,
what do you think I did? You will laugh at me – but
I got out and walked up. I did indeed. It might not be
saving them much, but it was something, and I could
not bear to sit at my ease, and be dragged up at the
expense of those noble animals. I caught a dreadful
cold, but that I did not regard." (20)

Mrs Norris is telling Sir Thomas that she has sacrificed the old coachman – and the horses – in her
devoted service to his interests, a devotion for which,
as the last detail in her speech makes clear, she has
been prepared to punish herself. Mrs Norris makes
others (like the old coachman) pay for her own
dependency and frustration, while, as John Wiltshire points out, "being able to hide this from herself
in the guise of generosity to the recipients and loyal
service to the system".

When Fanny arrives at Mansfield, her situation
has parallels with Mrs Norris's: both are single and
vulnerable, neither is part of the household except
by courtesy. While one lives in the small White
House, on the edge of the estate, the other lives in
the little white attic at the top of the house. So
Fanny becomes a scapegoat, one on whom Aunt
Norris can project, says Wiltshire, "the worth-
lessness, inferiority and indebtedness she is so
anxious to deny in herself... Fanny is humiliated
and punished, made to fetch and carry, scolded and
victimised, deprived of heat in the East room, so

that Mrs Norris can momentarily appease her own sense of functionless dependence." Mrs Norris, it might be added, can't show the resentment she feels towards her sister, Lady Bertram – but she can make up for it by inflicting as much misery as possible on Fanny.

It is by one of her spiteful stipulations that Fanny is not allowed a fire in the East room, and it is only when Sir Thomas visits the room to talk to his niece about Henry Crawford that this edict is revoked; he finds Fanny sitting by an empty grate although there is snow on the ground outside. Yet while Mrs Norris's villainy is obvious – she misses no opportunity to humiliate Fanny – what is less conspicuous is that her offences are condoned, permitted, sometimes even requested, by Sir Thomas. In Chapter One he directs her to help maintain the superior "rank, fortune, rights, and expectations" of his daughters at Fanny's expense; he approves Maria's marriage with a great family; he has never bothered to find out that Fanny has no fire in her room. Miss Norris is "less a villain in her own right than an adjutant", says Claudia Johnson. "In her, we see his officiousness, his liberality, his family pride, and even his parsimoniousness – after all, his anxieties about money make him wish Mrs Norris would take Fanny off his hands..."

When Aunt Norris denounces Fanny's "little spirit of secrecy and independence, and nonsense", he doesn't notice, as the narrator points out, that he himself, in the East room, has just been "expressing the same sentiments [about Fanny] himself". At the end of the novel, it is true, he realises how blind he has been and acknowledges his sense of kinship with Mrs Norris – seeing her, at last, as "a part of himself" – but her voluntary banishment conveniently spares him the fate of being continually reminded of his failings. Austen, in Johnson's view, was wary of attacking "authority figures" too directly, preferring to invest Mrs Norris with "mythic loathsomeness" while making it possible for Sir Thomas, "as well as any reader so inclined, to save face by palming his offenses on to a female surrogate from the realm of the fairytale".

What effect does Portsmouth have on Fanny?

When Fanny moves to Portsmouth, she feels more isolated than ever. Sir Thomas sends her there hoping it will change her mind about Henry Crawford:

> he... wished her to be heartily sick of home before her visit ended; and that a little abstinence from the elegancies and luxuries of Mansfield Park, would bring her mind to a sober state... It was a medicinal project upon his niece's understanding, which he must consider as at present diseased. (37)

The medical metaphors, says John Wiltshire, show how coercion, as often with Sir Thomas, is disguised "in the mask of kindness". Fanny receives his proposal to go to Portsmouth with rapture: "it seemed as if to be home again, would heal every pain that had since grown out of the separation [from it]".

Sir Thomas's assessment, though, is shrewder. Her Portsmouth home turns out to be a place of incessant noise, bad air, dirty crockery, bad manners and neglect. Fanny comes quickly to realise that Mansfield is her true home and to feel a sense of psychological exile. This is reflected in the startling modern sense of nausea she feels when considering the squalor of her mother's house:

She sat in a blaze of oppressive heat, in a cloud of moving dust; and her eyes could only wander from the walls marked by her father's head, to the table cut and knotched by her brothers, where stood the tea-board never thoroughly cleaned, the cups and saucers wiped in streaks, the milk a mixture of motes floating in thin blue, and the bread and butter growing every minute more greasy than even Rebecca's hands had first produced it. (46)

As Kingsley Amis once put it, "nice things are nicer than nasty things", and minutely observed scenes like this underline the way Fanny yearns for Mansfield Park and misses its comforts. "It is the assault which Portsmouth offers on the carefully charted boundaries of self that forces Fanny to recognise how identified that self is with a particular habitation, and how necessary its boundaries are," says Kathryn Sutherland. Fanny's yearning for Mansfield, which she comes to see as her true home, is a Romantic yearning; it is what Sutherland calls "a turn-of-the-century anxiety for connectedness"; we see it acutely in the search to belong which characterises the orphaned heroes of Dickens and Charlotte Brontë:

> *When she had been coming to Portsmouth, she had loved to call it her home, had been fond of saying that she was going home; the word had been very dear to her; and so it still was, but it must be applied to Mansfield. That was now the home. Portsmouth was Portsmouth; Mansfield was home. (45)*

When the "uncommitted self" finally chooses its "home", says Tony Tanner, it is in effect identifying with a certain way of life and a role within it. Throughout Henry James's *The Portrait of a Lady*, the heroine, Isabel Archer, is inspecting houses to see whether she can find one she can call home (though her final choice, Osmond's sterile little palace of art, proves a terrible error). Fanny's real, spiritual home is Mansfield. Early on in the novel, when it is suggested she goes to live with Mrs Norris, Lady Bertram says to her: "It can make little difference to you, whether you are in one house or the other." But when houses represent "edifices of value", in Tanner's phrase, it makes all the difference in the world. And Fanny's sense of alienation in Portsmouth is made clear in prose which is among the most violent Austen ever used. People "rush" and "push", children "squabble" and "kick"; the "smallness of the house" is emphasised, as is the "thinness of the walls"; everybody is always in everybody else's way; noise and movement are constant.

Yet homes in this novel, for the female characters, have to be found: they are not the houses into which they are born. Fanny's sense that Mansfield Park is where she belongs, and her rejection of her birthplace, mirror the Bertram daughters' growing dissatisfaction with their paternal abode. As Jane Stabler puts it:

> Domestic space defined the existence of middle-class women in Austen's day: whereas her male characters vacillate between different professions, most of her female characters face a future within four walls, whether they marry or not.

Maria marries dim Mr Rushworth because, says the narrator, "she was less and less able to endure the restraint which her father imposed... She must escape from Mansfield as soon as possible." When her marriage collapses, Julia panics: "imagining its certain consequences to herself would be greater severity and restraint", and "in increased dread of her father and of home", she elopes with the vacuous Mr Yates. All three cousins thus experience similar feelings of despair at the thought of being trapped in the place where they were born.

The other unmarried girl in the novel, Mary Crawford, is equally unsettled. Brought up by the disreputable Admiral, she is acutely aware of the misery that can be inflicted by a domineering husband or guardian and of the injuries done to her "poor, ill-used aunt". She sees, too, that her sister's husband, Dr Grant, is

> *an indolent selfish bon vivant, who must have his palate consulted in every thing, who will not stir a finger for the convenience of any one, and who, moreover, if the cook makes a blunder, is out of humour with his excellent wife. (11)*

The way Mary wields her charm, says Stabler, is understandable as a reaction against all "the petty manifestations of masculine tyranny she has witnessed". Like Fanny, Maria and Julia, she is looking for a stable, happy home.

But while Fanny longs for Mansfield, it is not the perfect haven she thinks it is, as Austen makes very clear, and while in Portsmouth she idealises it. On the surface, Portsmouth and Mansfield couldn't be more different. Portsmouth, for all the squalor of Fanny's parents' home, is bursting with life, and through the riotous energy of Fanny's brothers "hallooing in the passage", this scene of domestic chaos, says Stabler, represents the driving force of early 19th century society. Portsmouth is at the hub of the naval action against Napoleon and its dockyard is a source of national pride and excitement. Even the worldly Henry Crawford has visited Portsmouth "again and again".

Fanny is determined to see Mansfield and Portsmouth as diametrically opposed, but she's wrong, as subtle parallels between her experience in the two places suggest. Sir Thomas's exercise of "absolute power" is echoed in Mr Price's view, when he hears of Maria's elopement, that if she "belonged" to him he would "give her the rope's end as long as [he] could stand over her". In Northamptonshire, Dr Grant asks Edmund to "eat his mutton with him" and Fanny barely has time "for an unpleasant feeling on the occasion" before her company is asked for too. This is echoed in Portsmouth when Fanny's father asks Henry Crawford "to do them the honour of taking his mutton with them". Mary has only time "for one thrill of horror" before Henry graciously declines.

The squabble between Fanny's sisters over a silver knife echoes the Bertram sisters' fight to possess Henry, and Fanny's hapless mother reminds us of Lady Bertram's passivity. "Her disposition was naturally easy and indolent, like Lady Bertram's," the narrator tells us; they are linked too, we are told, by the "soft monotony" of their voices.

The dockyard scenes, says Stabler, dramatise the raw noise and action of British commerce and industry and of the war, which are "kept at a distance at Mansfield, but which provide all the comforts there". Fanny tries to import Mansfield culture to Portsmouth, joining a library, sitting upstairs to avoid "disturbance" and buying her own "biscuits and buns". To survive her inhospitable surroundings she builds up a compensating fantasy picture of Mansfield as perfect. She tries to shape Susan's mind, through reading and conversation, just as Edmund has shaped hers, and turns Susan into the second self who will eventually become "the stationary niece" responsible for "the hourly comforts of her aunt".

How important are objects in *Mansfield Park?*

"Things", and the way they circulate, matter in this novel. In Chapter Two we see the Bertram sisters "wasting gold paper"; Fanny, on the other hand, has no "writing materials" and can't send a letter to her brother; Edmund gives her what she needs; he brings her a glass of Madeira to soothe a headache, and wins her devotion by sending William a gold coin. The presents are all important in establishing the relationship.

When Mary Crawford comes to rehearse with Fanny, she notices the size of the chairs in the east room:

*"We must have two chairs at hand for you to bring
forward to the front of the stage. There – very good
school-room chairs, not made for a theatre, I dare
say; much more fitted for little girls to sit and kick
their feet against when they are learning a lesson."*

(18)

Later, when William and Henry Crawford leave the
house together and Fanny is left to cry in peace
over the remains of the breakfast table, Sir Thomas
believes "perhaps that the deserted chair of each
young man might exercise her tender enthusiasm,
and that the remaining cold pork bones and mus-
tard in William's plate might but divide her feelings
with the broken egg-shells in Mr Crawford's" (29).

These objects are dropped into the narrative
quietly, almost casually. "*Mansfield Park* contains no
accessory as visible as Robinson Crusoe's hairy hat
and umbrella, the writing materials of Richardson's
heroines, Oliver Twist's porridge bowl, or the sticks
and bicycles of Beckett's people," says Barbara
Hardy in "The objects in *Mansfield Park*". Austen
doesn't give objects as much significance as George
Eliot or Henry James, two novelists she strongly
influenced. Sotherton is heavy like its owner, faces
the wrong way and is badly in need of improvement,
but the symbolism is less evident than it is in, say,
The Portrait of a Lady, where Osmond's house is
portrayed in similar terms to him – small, jealous
and cruel. In *Middlemarch*, Dorothea, in her misery,
looks round her boudoir with "the shrunken

furniture, the never-read books... Each remembered thing in the room was disenchanted, was deadened as an unlit transparancy..."

There is no passage like this in *Mansfield Park,* says Hardy. Yet Austen, "the quiet initiator of so much in nineteenth century fiction", liked to place her heroines in solitary rooms, as Eliot later did with Dorothea, and Fanny has a store of precious objects which help her endure hard times. Austen constantly refers to the east room at Mansfield, which becomes very much Fanny's room, taking its stamp from her. Once used for lessons, it was for some time "quite deserted" we are told,

> *except by Fanny, when she visited her plants, or wanted one of the books... but gradually, as her value for the comforts of it increased, she had added to her possessions, and spent more of her time there; and having nothing to oppose her, had so naturally and so artlessly worked herself into it, that it was now generally admitted to be her's... (16)*

In a sense, the east room is the heart of Mansfield Park. Fanny returns to it time and again for comfort. "She could go there after any thing unpleasant below, and find immediate consolation..." Surveying her "nest of comforts" she thinks how valuable her possessions are to her:

> *...though she had known the pains of tyranny, of ridicule, and neglect, yet almost every recurrence of*

either had led to something consolatory... Edmund
had been her champion and friend; – he had
supported her cause, or explained her meaning, he
had told her not to cry, or had given her some proof
of affection which made her tears delightful. (16

Hardy calls this room "the archive of Mansfield Park": "its objects are the cast-offs of childhood, cared for only by Fanny". Like the Romantic hero of Wordsworth's *Prelude*, "she preserves the past with love, care, and imagination, willing life, never death". The "discarded childhoods" of the house are preserved in the relics. A few are carefully listed:

a faded footstool of Julia's work, too ill done for the
drawing room, three transparencies... where Tintern
Abbey held its station between a cave in Italy and a
moonlight lake in Cumberland... a small sketch of a
ship sent four years ago from the Mediterranean by
William, with H.M.S. Antwerp at the bottom, in
letter as tall as the main-mast.(16)

Memories are important to Fanny, who, in a scene of which Wordsworth would have approved, lectures a surprised Mary with uncharacteristic eloquence on the subject.

Opposite: Billie Piper as Fanny in the 2007 television adaptation

"If any one faculty of our nature may be called more wonderful than the rest, I do think it is memory... our powers of recollecting and of forgetting, do seem peculiarly past finding out." (22)

There is irony at work here, of course. Fanny cherishes the way objects in the East room evoke memories, and treasures her scrap of Edmund's letter, with the words "My dear Fanny", but to construct *Mansfield Park* as an ideal home, which she does while in Portsmouth, requires a talent for forgetting as well as remembering. The comforts of Mansfield, after all are equivocal: the rooms are large, their objects daunting; Fanny's room is cold; Mrs Norris is a tyrant.

Sometimes objects in the novel seem more symbolic. When Mary persuades Fanny to choose a necklace for the ball – and Fanny, reluctantly, makes her choice – Mary tells her the necklace was actually Henry's gift to her. Fanny instantly disavows the present.

Miss Crawford thought she had never seen a prettier consciousness. "My dear child," said she laughing, "what are you afraid of? Do you think Henry will claim the necklace as mine, and fancy you did not come honestly by it? – or are you imagining he would be too much flattered by seeing round your lovely throat an ornament which his money purchased three years ago, before he knew there was such a throat in the world? – or perhaps" – looking archly –

"you suspect a confederacy between us, and that what I'm now doing is with his knowledge and at his desire?" (26)

With deep blushes, Fanny denies this. To Mary, her "consciousness" must be the consciousness of desire for Henry and, indeed, it later becomes clear that Mary does think this. In fact Fanny blushes not through any desire for Henry but because she is embarrassed and feels she has been tricked. In the end, she doesn't wear the necklace for the ball because it doesn't fit through the amber cross she has been given by her brother. What does fit through the cross is a gold chain given by Edmund – "the only ornament" she has ever "had a desire to possess" – and it is this combination (of presents given by William and Edmund) that she ends up wearing.

Mary's casual way of thinking about "things" is very different from Fanny's. Her attitude to her accessories, says Barbara Hardy, "is carefully revealed as unimaginative, careless of the life around, whose routines make it amusingly inconvenient for a farmhouse to transport a young lady's harp" (brought to the parsonage, at her demand, during the harvest season). Mrs Norris's attitude to objects, more damningly, is entirely acquisitive. She sees them as spoils, sponging roses, or "supernumerary jellies" after Fanny's ball, or the green baize of the undrawn curtains for *Lovers' Vows*. She leaves Sotherton after the visit there heaving with goodies, including a cream cheese and some pheasant eggs, and from Mansfield itself she plunders an apricot sapling, roses from the garden, the green baize curtain from the play and probably the pink cloak too, which is last heard of in her possession.

Unlike Mrs Norris, Fanny learns to give and spend as well as receive, and she begins to do so in Portsmouth, just as it is there that she begins to teach (her sister Susan) as well as learn. She suddenly finds herself in a new position of power and responsibility, and able to heal a serious breach.

It had very early occurred to her, that a small sum of money might, perhaps, restore peace for ever on the sore subject of the silver knife... and the riches which she was in possession of herself, her uncle having given her £10 at parting, made her as able as she was willing to be generous. But she was so unpractised in removing evils, or bestowing kindnesses among equals, and so fearful of appearing to elevate herself as a great lady at home, that it took some time to determine that it would not be unbecoming in her to make such a present. It was made, however, at last.
(50)

She buys the knife, and food, and even books: "she became a subscriber – amazed at being anything in propria persona, amazed at her own doings in every way". In her early days at Mansfield, Tom describes the modest and dependent Fanny as a "creep-mouse", but now, says Hardy, the word ceases to be appropriate. She has grown out of being "a mere recipient". She has learned to give.

How deluded is Fanny?

What we make of *Mansfield Park* depends a great deal on what we make of its heroine. To Lionel Trilling and Tony Tanner it is not strong, repressed love that drives Fanny but moral rectitude. Another critic who all but ignores her passion is Harold Bloom. "Fanny as a will struggling only to be itself becomes at last the spiritual centre of Mansfield Park," he writes. "The quietest and most mundane of visionaries, she remains one of the firmest: her dedication is to the future of Mansfield Park as the idea of order it once seemed to her."

As John Wiltshire notes, these critics tend to see Fanny as Henry sees her – as a fantasy of female purity and goodness. Others, however, have come close to seeing her more as Mrs Norris sees her: as "the daemon of the piece". (If only she'd married Henry, Maria wouldn't have eloped and Mary might have married Edmund.) To the feminist critic Nina Auerbach, Fanny is a monster, a misanthropic hero-villain like Mary Shelley's *Frankenstein* or Byron's *Childe Harolde*.

Their flamboyant willfulness may seem utterly alien to this frail, clinging, and seemingly passive girl who annoys above all by her shyness, but like them, she is magnetically unconvivial, a spoiler of ceremonies. During the excursion to Sotherton, the rehearsals of *Lovers' Vows,* and the game of Speculation, her baleful solitude overwhelms the company, perhaps because it expresses and exudes her own buried rancour. In domestic set-ups ranging from Sir Thomas Bertram's stately authoritarianism to the casual disorder of her father's house, Fanny exists like Frankenstein as a silent, censorious pall. Her denying spirit defines itself best in assertive negatives: "No, indeed, I cannot act."

Auerbach, a critic of impeccable feminist credentials, dwells particularly on Fanny's almost anorexic dislike of food, noted frequently in the novel. "This denying girl," she writes,

> will not, perhaps cannot, eat. Home at Portsmouth, family food induces in her only a nausea that may be the most intense in 19th century fiction. Fanny's revulsion against food, along with her psychic feasting on the activities of others, associates her with that winsome predator the vampire, an equally solitary and melancholy figure who cannot eat the nourishment of daily life but who feasts secretly upon human vitality in the dark...

If she is Dracula, sucking the life out of Mansfield, Fanny is also "Jane Austen's *Hamlet,* scourge and minister of a corrupted world, the perfection of the character who won't play". Nobody in the novel really falls for her (Henry's passion is short-lived); her parents seem relieved when she leaves Portsmouth after her penitential visit; back at Mansfield she is embraced only "as a last resource when Sir Thomas's natural children disgrace themselves in turn". Austen, says Auerbach, is coolly explicit "about the cannibalistic undercurrents of this, and perhaps of all, requited love". The narrator writes:

My Fanny indeed at this very time, I have the satisfaction of knowing, must have been happy in spite of every thing. She must have been a happy creature in spite of all that she felt or thought she felt, for the distress of those around her... and happy as all this must make her, she would still have been happy without any of it, for Edmund was no longer the dupe of Miss Crawford.

It is true, that Edmund was very far from happy himself. He was suffering from disappointment and regret, grieving over what was, and wishing for what could never be. She knew it was so, and was sorry; but it was with a sorrow so founded on satisfaction, so tending to ease, and so much in harmony with every dearest sensation, that there are few who might not have been glad to exchange their greatest gaiety for it. (48)

Surely, says Auerbach, there is deliberate irony in Austen's repetition of the word "happy" in this description of a household of collapsed hopes. "Never in the canon is the happy ending so reliant upon the wounds and disappointment of others..." The love she wins is nothing but "the last tender impulse of a stricken household".

The love of her two suitors, in Auerbach's view, is similarly undermined. Henry Crawford is insincere, stages his love scenes before select audiences, puts as much public pressure on Fanny as he can, then humiliates her by eloping with Maria once she has begun to respond. As Fanny and we know, his passion for her is just a repetition of his wooing of her silly cousins: "in exposing the ardor of the romantic hero as a sadistic game, Jane Austen undermines the reader's own impulse to fall in love with Fanny by undermining love itself," says Auerbach.

But if Henry's love is just another variant of private theatricals, Edmund's love "is so restrained as to be almost imperceptible". He shows not the slightest jealousy when Henry Crawford proposes to his cousin. Austen is very good at describing men struggling with strong feeling: Knightley in *Emma*, Darcy in *Pride and Prejudice* and Wentworth in *Persuasion* all fight to repress love that proves too strong for them. There is no indication that Edmund feels anything half as strong as this. The narrator's perfunctory summary of his change of heart carries little emotional weight.

I only intreat every body to believe that exactly at the time when it was quite natural that it should be so, and not a week earlier, Edmund did cease to care about Mary Crawford, and became as anxious to marry Fanny, as Fanny herself could desire. (48)

This summary makes it hard to see Edmund as romantic or passionate. He is a limited figure, and his limitations are always clear. Mary Crawford tempts him sexually, and he responds. Austen "uses sexualised details more extensively here than in any other novel", says Claudia Johnson, and they attest to Edmund's susceptibility to "erotic enchantments". He encourages Mary's riding, as we have seen: her "pure genuine pleasure of the exercise" attracts him, and he delights in being "close to her... directing her management of the bridle". But while Edmund can accept Mary's unblushing vigour, he cannot, says Johnson, tolerate "what Darcy, so much the larger figure, finds so attractive in Elizabeth Bennet: her freedom of speech".

On hearing Mary complain of the admiral's messy improvements at Twickenham, Edmund is "silenced" by the free way she talks about her uncle: it "did not suit his sense of propriety". Her salacious joke about "Rears, and Vices", meets with an equally disapproving response. "Edmund again felt grave."

When Edmund, later, discusses with his pupil, Fanny, what was "not quite right" in Mary's conversation, they both agree that she "ought not to have spoken of her uncle as she did". "I do not censure his opinions; but there certainly is impropriety in making them public," says Edmund. Fanny goes further. She believes that it is not just Mary's expression of her sentiments that is wrong, but the sentiments themselves: "whatever his faults may be," she insists, he "is so very fond of her brother [Henry]" that he ought to be respected.* With Fanny, indeed, it is usually women who are at fault; she believes so strongly in the power of patricians that here she seeks to exculpate the

---

* This discussion between Edmund and Fanny is notable for its quasi-judicial language – acquit, censure, do justice to, blame. Judgement is very important in *Mansfield Park*: the word itself is used 37 times and the associated words (judge, judicious, just, justifiable, justly, justice, injustice, injudicious, injudiciously, unjust, unjustifiable, well-judging, ill-judged, ill-judging) make up a total of 116 occurrences in all.

COUNTRY HOUSE LITERATURE

Mansfield Park is part of a long tradition of English country house literature, going back to Ben Jonson's encomium to Sir Philip Sidney's birthplace, "To Penshurst" (1616), and continuing through John Dryden's "To My Honoured Kinsman John Driden" (1700) and Alexander Pope's "To Richard Boyle, Earl of Burlington" (1731). Common to these poems is praise of the house's modesty:

Thou art not, Penshurst, built to envious show, Of touch or marble; nor canst boast a row Of polished pillars, or a roof of gold;

A more important theme is the house's reciprocal relationship to its local community. In return for the tenants' labour and the wealth produced from the estate, the lord of the manor

admiral himself and blame his wife instead: "impropriety is a reflection itself upon Mrs Crawford... She cannot have given her [Mary] right notions of what was due to the admiral" (7).

To Claudia Johnson this is a revealing passage. Sir Thomas and Edmund are both limited figures who pursue their own selfish interests while disguising these to others, and to themselves, as moral imperatives. Edmund is kind to Fanny but he backs the plan to send her off to Mrs Norris when that is mooted; he wants her to take part in *Lovers' Vows*; and he tells her to marry Henry Crawford. "If it is true, as he proudly declares, that 'as the clergy are, or are not what they ought to be, so are the rest of the nation', then woe to England," says Claudia

would impose material, legal and even moral order, ensuring the well-being of the tenants, providing and maintaining their cottages, even acting as magistrate or justice of the peace.

The literary country house makes a late appearance in Evelyn Waugh's *A Handful of Dust* (1934), only now it's all gone wrong. Hetton Abbey, a huge pile in unfashionably showy Victorian Gothic, is the beloved family estate of Tony Last – appropriately named, since he will prove to be the last in his line when his only son is killed in a riding accident.

Tony himself (though not his wife Brenda) still puts in an appearance at the local parish church, where the vicar reiterates the stock sermon he gave while posted on the outskirts of empire. Meanwhile, Brenda, who is having an affair with an impoverished adventurer, wants to divorce Tony and live in London.

Mansfield Park is right on the cusp of this shift from feudal to modern. Like Penshurst, it is also compared favourably with more pretentious country houses such as Mr. Rushworth's family

Johnson.

Fanny, for her part, has so thoroughly internalised the lessons Edmund has taught her – has come so strongly to believe in Mansfield Park – that she accepts the flawed patriarchal system it represents while remaining blind to its faults. "The plot of *Mansfield Park* corroborates Fanny's severity with Mary Crawford, but at the same time it also explodes her confidence in the dispositions of patriarchal figures," says Johnson. To Nina Auerbach, Fanny's integration into Mansfield makes her a traitor to the feminist cause – a quiet, seemingly passive girl who ultimately opts to support those very patriarchal values which have oppressed her.

seat, Sotherton, with its various "improvements". On their visit there the young people find the road leading up the house in fine repair, but the tenants' cottages ruinous. The grounds are laid out rigidly to mathematical dimensions rather than to conform to the landscape. The family no longer hold household prayers, a subject of some debate in Chapter Nine.

But it's really the house after which the novel is named that's under scrutiny. Mansfield Park no longer has a lord of the manor; he's away in Antigua. Instead of tenants round about, involved in reciprocal economic, social and legal relationships with Mansfield, the estate's income is derived from slaves on a faraway sugar plantation, who get no benefits in return.

This all comes out in the irony of the children's geography lessons. The Bertram children are amused and appalled that Fanny "cannot tell the principal rivers in Russia" and has "never heard of Asia Minor", while they themselves know nothing of Antigua – where it is, what goes on there, and how it bears on their own moral and physical economy. ∎

Others are less severe. Fanny is a girl driven by love, but one who always tries to act, to feel, to imagine, as she has been directed; she even, says John Wiltshire, tries to make what she says to herself "a replication of what Sir Thomas and Edmund, were they privy to her desires, might say". Fighting her jealousy of Mary, and her longing for Edmund, she tells herself that the idea of thinking of him as anything other than a friend "ought not to have touched the confines of her imagination" – an arresting phrase. But the narrator sometimes asks for understanding.

She had all the heroism of principle, and was determined to do her duty; but having also many of the feelings of youth and nature, let her not be much wondered at if, after making all these good resolutions on the side of self-government, she seized the scrap of paper on which Edmund had begun writing to her... and... locked it up with the chain, as the dearest part of the gift.

There is something pathetic and comic in Fanny's "private intensities", as Wiltshire says – she is still very young – and the phrase "heroism of principle" is tinged with irony. In general, Fanny is "offered as a model of right behaviour, whilst simultaneously she is explored as a misguided, though well-intentioned and scrupulous product of a specific social and personal history". She loves Edmund. He may not be worthy of her love but she never repudiates her feelings or gives up on him. Deluded as she is, she is not a weak character but, contrary to appearances, a very strong one.

How believable is the ending of *Mansfield Park*?

Jane Austen "was a great enough novelist to put more than one truth in a book", says her biographer, Claire Tomalin. On one level, *Mansfield Park* can be read as a defence of conservative rural values. Many critics have read it as such. Sir Thomas is shocked into realising how badly he has mismanaged his family and undervalued Fanny. Tom, too, is reformed – by his illness. "He had suffered and he had learnt to think, two advantages that he had never known before... He became what he ought to be, useful to his father, steady and quiet, not living for himself."

But on another level *Mansfield Park* is more subversive. D.W. Harding, who was a professional psychologist as well as a regular contributor to the Cambridge critical magazine, Scrutiny, argued in 1939 that Austen's novels reveal fear and hatred of the mocked characters and of society generally. Among the targets of her rage is the situation of women in the gentry.

Mrs Norris, Sir Thomas's sister-in-law and Fanny's principal tormentor, is treated with scathing sarcasm from the beginning. But the novel also provides us with all the material we need for a devastating view of the vegetable Lady Bertram on her sofa while simultaneously showing us that Fanny herself never entertains such a view. When Tom falls dangerously ill, Fanny, still in Portsmouth, is distressed and anxious to help, though she can't repress her own private anxiety about Edmund and Mary Crawford. After the first letter from Lady Bertram we read:

Fanny's feelings on the occasion were indeed considerably more warm and genuine than her aunt's style of writing. She felt truly for them all. Tom dangerously ill, Edmund gone to attend him, and the sadly small party remaining at Mansfield, were cares to shut out every other care, or almost every other. She could just find selfishness enough to wonder whether Edmund had written to Miss Crawford before his summons came, but no sentiment dwelt long with her, that was not purely affectionate and disinterestedly anxious. Her aunt did not neglect her; she wrote again and again; they were receiving frequent accounts from Edmund, and these accounts were as regularly transmitted to Fanny, in the same diffuse style, and the same medley of trusts, hopes, and fears, all following and producing each other at hap-hazard. It was a sort of playing at being frightened. (44)

This passage is a mixture of free indirect speech

and narrative comment. As Roy Pascal notes, the early phrases "Tom dangerously ill" and "She could just find selfishness enough" are clearly free indirect speech – they are Fanny's thoughts; only she could call her concern for Edmund "selfish". But the later comments on the "diffuse style" and the "medley of trusts, hopes, and fears" in Lady Bertram's letters, as well as the sharp last sentence, are the narrator's own. "Does Fanny allow herself to notice that Lady Bertram, good-natured as she is, is indolent, easy-going and selfish?" asks Pascal. The answer is no. Decisive criticism of Lady Bertram is allowed only to the narrator.

Just as Fanny's faith in *Mansfield Park* is frequently undercut, so is the conservative, patriarchal vision the novel on the surface upholds. The last chapter plays, in a brilliantly witty but chilling way, with the whole idea of a God-like novelist dispensing justice. In so doing it forces us to question what we read. In Claudia Johnson's apposite summary:

> From the Bertrams' point of view, the novel closes with a vengeance of reactionary formulas derived from conservative fiction: the demon aunt is cast out as a betrayer of the good man's trust, and the offending daughter banished to the hell of her perpetual company; the impious seductress is righteously spurned by the man of God, and her reprobate brother forever barred from happiness; the giddy heir apparent is

sobered by instructive affliction, and the modest girl, in a triumph of passive aggression, is vindicated and rewarded with everything she wanted but never presumed to ask for.

The wicked are not merely segregated from the virtuous; the virtuous huddle together with Sir Thomas, who, "anxious to bind by the strongest securities all that remained to him of domestic felicity", repents his past ways and blesses the marriage of Edmund and Fanny. This ending is almost a parody, says Johnson; by "hurrying her characters to tidy destinies" Austen "lurches the novel into fantasies we are not permitted to credit". The overall effect is to undermine the conventionally happy ending.

Living in her parents' squalid home in Portsmouth, it seemed to Fanny that "all proceeded in a regular course of cheerful orderliness" at Mansfield, that "everybody had their due importance; everybody's feelings were consulted". But this, as we know, was never true. Mansfield Park was never "cheerful" or orderly and "everyone's" feelings there were not consulted, Fanny's least of all. Yet in the last paragraph of the novel we are told that for Fanny everything at Mansfield Park, including her uncle's patronage, had long been "thoroughly perfect".

We can't be expected to take this too seriously. Nor are we encouraged to make too much of Maria's offence. "Although Austen writes nothing that can be construed as a palliation of adultery, the narrator shows no ladylike impulse to recoil in shame from the greatest insult that can be made to a man of Rushworth's prestige," says Claudia Johnson. Not only does the narrator imply that Rushworth had it coming – "The indignities of stupidity, and the disappointments of selfish passion, can excite little pity. His punishment followed his conduct" – but suggests that he may be betrayed again – "if duped, to be duped at least with good humour and good luck".

If the novel's instance of illicit sex doesn't rouse much indignation, "its instance of licit sex is less than exemplary as well", says Johnson. The match between Edmund and Fanny savours of incest. It is perfectly legal – first cousins were allowed to marry (they still are) – but the closeness of the family tie is constantly stressed, with Sir Thomas early on expressing opposition to "cousins in love, &c" and Mrs Norris saying that it is "morally impossible" for cousins to marry who have been "always together like brothers and sisters". Sir Thomas later arranges Henry's abrupt departure in the hope of making Fanny feel his absence "con amore".

She does feel it, but only because William goes too: "it was con amore fraternal and no other". In the enclosed world of Mansfield Park, choice is limited and fraternal ties are very important. Conscious of this, Henry, seeking to take advantage of Fanny's attachment to her brother, William, shrewdly presses his suit immediately after arranging William's promotion. He hopes her affections can be transferred from William to him.

And they might have been, as the narrator points out in the last chapter. If circumstances had been different, if Henry had persisted, Fanny would have "voluntarily bestowed" herself on him, and if Mary hadn't spoken so flippantly in her last scene with Edmund, things might have turned out differently for everyone.

What view of the world does *Mansfield Park* leave us with?

Jane Austen's political views are hard to pin down, though on some subjects they are clear enough. There is no doubt, for example, that she opposed slavery. Her naval brother wrote sternly about the wrongs of the slave trade in his Notebook of 1808; Austen must have been aware of the "Mansfield Judgement" which gave slaves the right of *Habeas Corpus* and ruled that black slaves brought to England must immediately be freed on the grounds that English air was "too pure for slaves to breathe in". This verdict was echoed by William Cowper in *The Task* (1785), one of Fanny's – and Austen's – favourite poems, when he wrote:

Slaves cannot breathe in England; if their lungs
Receive our air, that moment they are free...

The abolition of slavery was one of the main aims of the progressive Evangelical wing of the Anglican Church, and Austen may have been sympathetic not just to its anti-slavery campaign but to the broader aims of this movement. As a number of critics, including the influential Marilyn Butler, have pointed out, Fanny and Edmund come close to propounding the Evangelical message in *Mansfield Park*.

The daughter of a clergyman, Austen took a keen interest in the Evangelicals, a movement which included morally conservative campaigners like William Wilberforce and Hannah More. At about the time of *Mansfield Park*'s publication in 1814, Austen's niece, Fanny Knight, was considering marriage to James Plumtre, but was deterred by his "Goodness" and "the danger of his becoming an Evangelical". Austen advised her not to worry: "I am by no means convinced that we ought not all to be Evangelicals," she wrote – a sign that, despite reservations, she had some sympathy with the movement. She would have been aware of what Edmund calls the "spirit of improvement abroad" as the Anglican Church responded to criticism from the likes of Wilberforce and More. Hannah More, in fact, wanted to reform not just the clergy but English secular life too: "this world is not a stage for the display of superficial talents," she wrote (as if with the Crawfords in mind), " but for the strict and sober exercise of fortitude, temperance, meekness, faith, diligence and self-denial".

Central to the Evangelical concept of the Good Life, says Kathryn Sutherland in her introduction to the Penguin *Mansfield Park,* was the importance of reading. Fanny, a "revisionist Eve", is the heroine of a text which sees books as "morally influential and socially determining". "Against the notorious seductive power of *Lovers' Vows,* we need to set Fanny's favourite books: Cowper's poems, Johnson's *Idler,* and Crabbe's *Tales,* together representing a wholesome programme of edifying family reading."

In this readerly context, says Sutherland, the novel's re-working of *Paradise Lost* needs to be taken seriously. The famous Sotherton episode is, "in its distinctly feminised alignment of Christian and conservative values, a historically specific revision of Milton's interpretation of the temptation scene". Fanny's view of things at Sotherton from her fenced elevation in the gardens would have won Hannah More's approval. In her *Strictures on the Modern System of Female Education,* More writes:

A woman sees the world, as it were, from a little elevation in her own garden, whence she takes an exact survey of home scenes, but takes not in that wider range of distant prospects, which he who stands on a loftier eminence commands. Women often feel what is just more instantaneously than they can define it. They have an intuitive penetration into character, bestowed on them by Providence...

If, like the feminist writer Mary Wollstonecraft, Austen felt rage about the limitations women faced in society, she was also, like both Wollstonecraft and More, sympathetic to the view that educated women were better guardians of domestic life than men. In More's Evangelical view, young women of what Sutherland calls "the uncertain social middle", like Fanny, had the power to re-educate the "decadent upper ranks" and thus to stiffen the nation's moral spine and help it at a time of war.

The language of *Mansfield Park* often reflects the Evangelical belief in maintaining high standards and carefully examining what motivates us. Sir Thomas's realisation that "something must have been wanting within" his plan of education and that his children lacked "active principle" suggests the danger of shallow thinking (an Evangelical concern), while Fanny's constant questioning of whether she should act in *Lovers' Vows* – "Was she right in refusing... Was it not ill-nature – selfishness – and a fear of exposing herself?" – are in keeping with Wilberforce's injunction to Christians: "Scrutinise yourself... with rigorous strictness."

But while Christian Evangelical leanings supply an ideal to aspire to, neither Fanny nor Edmund live up to them. As Jane Stabler says, Fanny is caught between "all the heroism of principle" and her suppressed passion for her cousin, and her speech "veers accordingly between poetic sententiae, and more troubled evasions and hints". She eulogises about the beauties of nature to be found "sitting out of doors", but when she is actually left sitting out of doors at Sotherton she is less interested in nature than in what is happening between Mary and Edmund.

The tensions between her ideals and her passion also show in Portsmouth. Mary writes to her making a callously frank calculation about the effect of Tom's illness. Fanny, we are told in a subtle piece of free indirect narration, "felt more than justified" in informing Edmund of this. We also hear of Fanny's quiet "satisfaction" with Edmund's disappointment in Mary. Stabler writes:

> Fanny's battles against her instincts often end in failure, and she is far from being the angel Henry Crawford would like to force to love him, or the paragon of Evangelical virtue portrayed by later critics.

Instead Fanny exposes the fallibility of Evangelical doctrines – showing how easily they can be derailed by strong feeling. Fanny's understanding of what goes on around her is never more than partial, and her memory, as we have seen, is highly selective. The way Austen uses free indirect speech in *Mansfield Park,* allowing us to see things from all sorts of points of view, reinforces this. Fanny is a romantic, but to think of Mansfield Park and Sir Thomas as bastions of morality and decency requires not just a selective memory but a good deal of self-deception.

Without realising it, says John Wiltshire, Fanny is a victim of "the patriarchal conception" of women as "commodities", a point which becomes clear, for example, when she "comes out" at her ball. Her coming out has been discussed since Mary Crawford asks, soon after her arrival: "Pray, is she out, or not out?"* But when the ball finally happens the narrator makes plain her disaste for the ritual:

Miss Price, known only by name to half the people invited, was now to make her first appearance, and must be regarded as Queen for the evening. Who could be happier than Miss Price? But Miss Price had not been brought up to the trade of coming out...
(27)

The tone here recalls the feminist Mary Wollstonecraft.

What can be more indelicate than a girl's coming out in the fashionable world? Which, in other

---

* Ruth Yeazell thinks Mary's question sheds light on her character. "By presuming that the only alternative to the girl who abruptly alters her behaviour when she comes out is the girl who acts immodestly from the start, Mary unwittingly reveals that she finds a modest consciousness unimaginable. All she can recognise is the difference between manners and appearance, the distinction between acting with and without restraint."

words, is to bring to market a marriageable miss, whose person is taken from one public place to another, richly caparisoned...

The paradox between Fanny's romanticism, and the way she is treated, says Wiltshire,

> is captured in the novel's shifts of tone, between the tender sympathy with which Fanny's consciousness is represented, and the surrounding narrative's worldly and astringent irony, which enacts the fact that Fanny is enclosed within a society whose harsher imperatives cannot be indefinitely refused.

The worldliness is clear throughout the novel. The Ward sisters are disposed of in marriage as if at an auction, while Maria's loveless marriage, as D.W. Harding notes, is "made in full accord with the ethos which saw marriage as a move in the business of economic and social bargaining between the country families". It is exactly parallel with the metropolitan marriage of Mary Crawford's friend Janet Fraser, and the parallel "fundamentally modifies" any simple contrast between the metropolitan code and the code of Mansfield Park.

That the division between rural Mansfield and corrupt London is not as sharp as critics like Tony Tanner allege it to be is clear from the treatment of the Crawfords. They are manipulative and cynical, but their openly affectionate manner towards one another has a warmth noticeably lacking at Mansfield. Mary is capable of being kind-hearted and Henry, as Harding says, shows "genuine good feeling and tact" in dealing with Fanny in the midst of her dreadful family in Portsmouth. "However improbable his falling in love with her may remain, the good qualities that make his possible reform not quite inconceivable are conveyed convincingly."

Nature matters as well as nurture. One condition necessary for "moral development", says Harding, may be the inculcation of a satisfactory moral code and the provision of good personal examples in early life. This the Crawfords lacked, in particular the principle that immediate pleasure sometimes has to be sacrificed to duty. But "training in good principles is not enough". There needs also to be "good natural quality" in the individual. Tom and Edmund are both exposed to Mansfield training, such as it is, but differing in personality they "grow up into morally different people" (though Tom, it is true, is chastened by his illness). Fanny, in Portsmouth, takes Susan in hand and is surprised by what she finds.

Her greatest wonder on the subject soon became – not that Susan should have been provoked into disrespect and impatience against her better knowledge – but that so much better knowledge, so many good notions, should have been hers at all; and that, brought up in the midst of negligence and error, she should have formed such proper opinions of what ought to be – she, who had no cousin

Edmund to direct her thoughts or fix her principles.
(41)

Much of the novel is set in an enclosed country house world. While Darcy in *Pride and Prejudice* looks beyond Pemberley for his bride, the family circle at the end of *Mansfield Park* huddles together. There is no injection of reinvigorating new blood. Fanny herself is an isolated figure, and her isolation is never fully dissolved. Through most of the narrative she feels homesick, first at Mansfield, then in Portsmouth, and her happiness, when it comes, is at the expense of others. She is a less appealing figure than Austen's other heroines, and never truly loved. The man she marries is less engaging, and an altogether smaller figure than Darcy or Mr Knightley in *Emma* or Wentworth in *Persuasion*.

Though often seen as a novel which champions family life it is also one which raises disturbing questions about families. Henry calls marriage "Heaven's last best gift", while his sister says: "there is not one in a hundred of either sex, who is not taken in when they marry... it is, of all transactions, the one in which people expect most from others, and are least honest themselves" (5). Besides the example of her aunt and uncle, Mary has seen her friends, one after the other, enter into loveless marriages.[*]

[*]   The Stornaways, the Frasers and the Aylmers are all briefly but significantly mentioned.

Mother and daughter relationships, usually fraught if not non-existent in Jane Austen, are here almost negligible. Maria and Julia take no notice of their mother; Fanny feels little for hers, and vice versa. ("Her daughters had never been much to her."/"[Fanny] did feel that her mother was a partial, ill-judging parent, a dawdle, a slattern...") Fathers, uncles and guardians are similarly inadequate. Maria and Julia fall out; Fanny's sisters are not close. In *Mansfield Park* the only real love given credence is the love between sister and brother; in Fanny's case between sister and brother and sister and foster brother. However, the final image of Edmund and Fanny sheltering each other "within the view and patronage of Mansfield Park" provides the most fragile of consolations, says Kathryn Sutherland. Fanny has returned to find a family in ruins, but this distress, as the narrator points out, is the foundation of her happiness. "She must have been a happy creature in spite of all that she felt or thought she felt, for the distress of those around her." How can Fanny not be happy, asks Sutherland

amid so much real distress, when previously she was anguished amid so much seeming good fortune and security? The novel poses several such disturbing questions, the cumulative effect of which is to challenge the very values (of tradition, stability, retirement, and faithfulness) it appears to endorse.

Often seen as a Cinderella story, *Mansfield Park* is perhaps more justly compared to *King Lear*. As Jane Stabler says, this novel, like Shakespeare's play, is a story of an archetypal father figure who loses his authority by over-estimating two of his daughters and under-estimating the youngest. Goneril and Regan fight for Edmund just as Julia and Maria fight for Henry; Cordelia rejects Lear's auctioning of her affection as Fanny stubbornly refuses to the transaction proposed by Sir Thomas; she is banished, but eventually recognised by Sir Thomas as "the daughter that he wanted".

Small but important details suggest that Austen had Lear in mind. More than once, Fanny is charged with "ingratitude", the sin Lear fears most in his offspring, and when Edmund advises Fanny to let Henry "succeed at last" she bursts out: "Oh! never, never, never; he will never succeed with me" – an echo of Lear's final despairing negatives.

> Thou'lt come no more,
> Never, never, never, never, never! (V.iii)

Mansfield Park is Austen's bleakest study of human relationships, of how incompatible people's aims and interpretations of events can be and of how little understanding often exists within families. "Is there any cause in nature which makes these hard hearts?" asks Lear. It is a question which Austen also seems to be asking in *Mansfield Park*.

BIBLIOGRAPHY

Baker, William, *A Critical Companion to Jane Austen; A Literary Reference to Her Life and Work*, Facts On File, 2007

Bautz, Annika (ed.), *Jane Austen: A Reader's Guide to Essential Criticism*, Palgrave Macmillan, 2010

Butler, Marilyn, *Jane Austen and the War of Ideas*, OUP, 1975

Byrne, Paula, *Jane Austen's Emma, A Sourcebook,* Routledge, 2004

Chapman, R.W. (ed.), *The Novels of Jane Austen*, Clarendon, 1923

Cookson, Linda/Loughrey, Bryan (eds.), *Critical Essays on Emma*, Longman, 1988

Craik, W.A., *Jane Austen: The Six Novels*, Methuen & Co, 1965

Cunningham, Valentine, *In the Reading Gaol*, Blackwell, 1994

Duckworth, Alistair, *Emma: Case Studies*, Palgrave, 2001

Farnsworth, Rodney, *Mediating Order and Chaos*, Rodopi, 2002

Gilmour, Robin, *The Idea of the Gentleman in the Victorian Novel*, Allen and Unwin, 1981

Harding, D.W., *Regulated Hatred and Other Essays on Jane Austen*, Athlone Press, 1998

Johnson, Claudia, *Jane Austen: Women, Politics and the Novel*, University of Chicago Press, 1988

Leavis, F.R., *The Great Tradition*, Chatto & Windus, 1962

Miller, D.A., *Jane Austen, or The Secret of Style*, Princeton University Press, 2003

Mullan, John , *What Matters in Jane Austen? Twenty Crucial Puzzles Solved*, Bloomsbury, 2012

Neill, Edward, *The Politics of Jane Austen*, Macmillan, 1999

Parrish, Stephen (ed.), *Emma: A Norton Critical Edition*, W.W. Norton & Company, 2000

Prewitt Brown, Julia, *Jane Austen's Novels: Social Change and Literary Form*, Harvard University Press, 1979

Sales, Roger, *Jane Austen and Representations of Regency England*, Routledge, 1996

Stafford, Fiona (ed.), *Emma*, Penguin Classics edition, 1996

Tanner, Tony, *Jane Austen*, Harvard University Press, 1986

Todd, Janet, *The Cambridge Introduction to Jane Austen*, Cambridge University Press, 2006

Tomalin, Claire, *Jane Austen: A Life*, Penguin, 1997

Wright, Andrew, *Jane Austen's Novels: A Study in Structure*, Chatto & Windus, 1953

Bayley, John, "The 'Irresponsibility' of Jane Austen", from

Critical Essays on Jane Austen, ed. B.C. Southam, London, 1968

Booth, Wayne, "Point of View and Control of Distance in *Emma*", Nineteenth-Century Fiction, 16, 1961-62

Campbell, Suzie, "The significance of games in *Emma*", *Critical Essays on Emma*, Linda Cookson/Brian Loughrey (eds.), Longman, 1988

Fergus, Jan, "The Power of Women's Language and Laughter", *The Talk in Jane Austen*, ed. Bruce Stovel, Lynn Weinlos Gregg, University of Alberta Press, 2002

Ford, Susan Allen, "How to Read and Why: *Emma*'s Gothic Mirrors", *Persuasion*s Vol 25, 2003

Gibson, Andrew, "'Imaginism' and objectivity in *Emma*", *Critical Essays on Emma*, Linda Cookson/Brian Loughrey (eds.), Longman, 1988

Harris, Jocelyn, "Silent Women, Shrews, and Bluestockings", *The Talk in Jane Austen*, ed. Bruce Stovel/Lynn Weinlos Gregg, University of Alberta Press, 2002

Hayes, E.N., "*Emma*: a Dissenting Opinion", Nineteenth-Century Fiction, 4, 1949-50

Hollindale, Peter, "Age and Patronage in *Emma*", *Critical Essays on Emma*, Linda Cookson/Brian Loughrey (eds.), Longman, 1988

Kettle, Arnold, "Jane Austen: *Emma*", from *An Introduction to the English Novel*, Vol 1, London, 1951

Lascelles, Mary, *Jane Austen and Her Art*, Clarendon Press, 1939

Morgan, Susan, "Emma Woodhouse and the Charms of Imagination", Studies in the Novel, 7.1, Spring 1975

Parkinson, Kathleen, "Courtship and marriage in *Emma*", *Critical Essays on Emma*, Linda Cookson/Brian Loughrey (eds.), Longman, 1988

Pickrel, Paul, "Lionel Trilling and *Emma*: A Reconsideration", Nineteenth-Century Fiction, 40, 1985

Porter, Roy, *The Penguin Social History of Britain: English Society in the Eighteenth Century*, 1990

Rogers, J.E. Jr, "Emma Woodhouse: Betrayed by Place", *Persuasions* 21, 1999

Schorer, Mark, "The Humiliation of Emma Woodhouse", Literary Review, 2, 1959

Sutherland, Kathryn, "Jane Austen and the invention of the serious modern novel", *The Cambridge Companion to English Literature, 1740-1830*, Tom Keymer/Jon Mee (eds.), Cambridge University Press, 2004

Trilling, Lionel, "*Emma*", Encounter 8.6, June 1957

Watts, Cedric, "The Limitations of *Emma*", *Critical Essays on Emma*, Linda Cookson/Brian Loughrey (eds.), Longman, 1988

Watt, Ian, "Jane Austen and the Traditions of Comic Aggression", *Persuasions* 3, 1981

Wiltshire, John, "Emma", *The Cambridge Companion to Jane Austen*, Cambridge University Press, 1997

A SHORT CHRONOLOGY

1747 Samuel Richardson's *Clarissa*.

1771 John Broadwood produces his first square piano, further developing it in 1781.

1775 December 16th Jane Austen born in Steventon, Hampshire, to Revd. George and Cassandra Austen, the seventh of eight children, and the younger of two daughters.

1782 Frances Burney's *Cecilia*.

1783-1786 Austen attends boarding schools with her sister Cassandra in Oxford and Reading.

1787-1793 Austen writes various short works which she would later collect in three bound notebooks now known as the *Juvenilia*. These are often exercises in parody including *Love and Freindship* [sic.], a burlesque novel of sensibility, and her *History of England*, which comically satirised Oliver Goldsmith.

1789 Blake's *Songs of Experience*.

1790 Burke's *Reflections on the Revolution in France*.

1791 Thomas Paine's *The Rights of Man*.

1792 Mary Wollstonecraft's *Vindication of the Rights of Woman*.

1793 France declares war on Britain at the start of the French Revolutionary Wars. Louis XVI and Marie Antoinette executed.

1798 Wordsworth and Coleridge: *Lyrical Ballads.*

1803-1815 The Napoleonic Wars. Austen's brother, Francis, made a captain in the navy. He later becomes a rear admiral.

1805 Revd. George Austen dies; succeeded as rector at Steventon by his son James. Bill abolishes the slave trade to newly conquered islands. Slavery is abolished outright in 1833.

1809 Austen moves with her sister and mother to a cottage at Chawton owned by her brother Edward.

1811 *Sense and Sensibility* published. George III declared irretrievably mad, and his son made Prince Regent.

1812 Napoleon invades Russia. Britain at war with the United States.

1813 *Pride and Prejudice* published by Thomas Egerton.

1814 *Mansfield Park* published. Austen begins Emma.

1815 Jane is invited to admire Prince Regent's London residence at Carlton House by his librarian, James Stanier Clarke. The Prince suggests that Austen include him in the dedication of her next work. *Emma* is published in December by John Murray, and reviewed favourably by Sir Walter Scott in the *Quarterly Review.* Battle of Waterloo.

1817 July 18th Austen dies in Winchester and is buried in Winchester Cathedral. In December *Northanger Abbey* and *Persuasion* published posthumously, with 1818 on the title page.

1869 James Austen Leigh's *A Memoir of Jane Austen.*

INDEX

⦾ CONNELL GUIDES

Concise, intelligent guides to history and literature

CONNELL GUIDES TO LITERATURE

Novels and poetry
Emma
Far From the Madding Crowd
Frankenstein
Great Expectations
Hard Times
Heart of Darkness
Jane Eyre
Lord of the Flies
Mansfield Park
Middlemarch
Mrs Dalloway
Paradise Lost
Persuasion
Pride and Prejudice
Tess of the D'Urbervilles
The Canterbury Tales
The Great Gatsby
The Poetry of Robert Browning
The Waste Land
To Kill A Mockingbird
Wuthering Heights

Shakespeare
A Midsummer Night's Dream
Antony and Cleopatra
Hamlet
Julius Caesar

King Lear
Macbeth
Othello
Romeo and Juliet
The Second Tetralogy
The Tempest
Twelfth Night

Modern texts
A Doll's House
A Room with a View
A Streetcar Named Desire
An Inspector Calls
Animal Farm
Atonement
Beloved
Birdsong
Hullabaloo
Never Let Me Go
Of Mice and Men
Rebecca
Spies
The Bloody Chamber
The Catcher in the Rye
The History Boys
The Road
Vernon God Little
Waiting for Godot

First published in 2017 by
Connell Guides
Spye Arch House
Spye Park
Lacock
Chippenham
Wiltshire SN15 2PR

10 9 8 7 6 5 4 3 2 1

Picture credits:
p.31 © Everett Collection/ Rex Features
p.65 © Wikicommons
p.81 © Graham Wiltshire/ Getty Images

A CIP catalogue record for this book is available from the British Library.

ISBN 978-1-907776-30-4

Design © Nathan Burton
Printed in Great Britain

Assistant Editors:
Georgia McVeigh and Paul Woodward

www.connellguides.com